Mergers and Acquisitions

A National Bureau
of Economic Research
Project Report

Mergers and Acquisitions

Edited by   Alan J. Auerbach

The University of Chicago Press

Chicago and London

ALAN J. AUERBACH is a professor of economics at the University of Pennsylvania and a research associate of the National Bureau of Economic Research.

The University of Chicago Press, Chicago 60637
The University of Chicago Press, Ltd., London

Library of Congress Cataloging-in-Publication Data

Mergers and acquisitions.

  (A National Bureau of Economic Research project report)
  Includes bibliographies and index.
  1. Consolidation and merger of corporations—
Congresses. 2. Junk bonds—Congresses. 3. Consolidation and merger of corporations—Taxation—Congresses.
I. Auerbach, Alan J.   II. Series.
HD2746.5.M45   1988   658.1′6   87-19035
ISBN 0-226-03209-4

Relation of the Directors to the
Work and Publications of the
National Bureau of Economic Research

1. The object of the National Bureau of Economic Research is to ascertain and to present to the public important economic facts and their interpretation in a scientific and impartial manner. The Board of Directors is charged with the responsibility of ensuring that the work of the National Bureau is carried on in strict conformity with this object.

2. The President of the National Bureau shall submit to the Board of Directors, or to its Executive Committee, for their formal adoption all specific proposals for research to be instituted.

3. No research report shall be published by the National Bureau until the President has sent each member of the Board a notice that a manuscript is recommended for publication and that in the President's opinion it is suitable for publication in accordance with the principles of the National Bureau. Such notification will include an abstract or summary of the manuscript's content and a response form for use by those Directors who desire a copy of the manuscript for review. Each manuscript shall contain a summary drawing attention to the nature and treatment of the problem studied, the character of the data and their utilization in the report, and the main conclusions reached.

4. For each manuscript so submitted, a special committee of the Directors (including Directors Emeriti) shall be appointed by majority agreement of the President and Vice Presidents (or by the Executive Committee in case of inability to decide on the part of the President and Vice Presidents), consisting of three Directors selected as nearly as may be one from each general division of the Board. The names of the special manuscript committee shall be stated to each Director when notice of the proposed publication is submitted to him. It shall be the the duty of each member of the special manuscript committee to read the manuscript. If each member of the manuscript committee signifies his approval within thirty days of the transmittal of the manuscript, the report may be published. If at the end of that period any member of the manuscript committee withholds his approval, the President shall then notify each member of the Board, requesting approval or disapproval of publication, and thirty days additional shall be granted for this purpose. The manuscript shall then not be published unless at least a majority of the entire Board who shall have voted on the proposal within the time fixed for the receipt of votes shall have approved.

5. No manuscript may be published, though approved by each member of the special manuscript committee, until forty-five days have elapsed from the transmittal of the report in manuscript form. The interval is allowed for the receipt of any memorandum of dissent or reservation, together with a brief statement of his reasons, that any member may wish to express: and such memorandum of dissent or reservation shall be published with the manuscript if he so desires. Publication does not, however, imply that each member of the Board has read the manuscript, or that either members of the Board in general or the special committee have passed on its validity in every detail.

6. Publications of the National Bureau issued for informational purposes concerning the work of the Bureau and its staff, or issued to inform the public of activities of Bureau staff, and volumes issued as a result of various conferences involving the National Bureau shall contain a specific disclaimer noting that such publication has not passed through the normal review procedures required in this resolution. The Executive Committee of the Board is charged with review of all such publications

from time to time to ensure that they do not take on the character of formal research reports of the National Bureau, requiring formal Board approval.

7. Unless otherwise determined by the Board or exempted by the terms of paragraph 6, a copy of this resolution shall be printed in each National Bureau publication.

(Resolution adopted October 25, 1926, as revised through September 30, 1974)

Contents

Acknowledgments

This volume contains five papers that were originally presented at a National Bureau of Economic Research Conference on October 7, 1986, in New York. It represents a progress report on the National Bureau's research project on mergers and acquisitions, an undertaking that has been made possible through the generous support of the Seaver Institute.

This volume began with the flawless organization of the conference itself by Kirsten Foss Davis and Ilana Hardesty of the NBER. Stewart Myers and another, anonymous NBER research associate provided useful comments on the manuscript. Mark Fitz-Patrick and Annie Spillane, of the bureau's staff, have shepherded the book through the publication process.

The opinions expressed in this volume are those of the respective authors. They do not necessarily represent the views of the National Bureau of Economic Research, the Seaver Institute, or any other organization with which any of the authors may be affiliated.

Acknowledgments

Introduction

Alan J. Auerbach

What causes mergers and acquisitions, and how do they affect the economy? The recent wave of merger and takeover activity in the United States has led many leaders of business and government to ask these and related questions. Some have concluded that there are questionable motives for mergers and takeovers and often undesirable results. This has led to government attempts to discourage corporate combinations through financial and tax restrictions and to increases in the frequency and sophistication of antitakeover amendments to corporate charters.

Because there are many classes of individuals affected by any particular change in corporate control, it is difficult to draw conclusions about the costs and benefits of mergers and acquisitions without comprehensive examination. In the case of a takeover attempt, for example, one must consider the impact on the shareholders, the creditors, the employees, the management, and the customers of each company involved, as well as on competing firms and, through changes in tax revenue or default risk, taxpayers in general. Not every group will be helped by a given merger, but a commonly accepted criterion is that the outcome is socially desirable if the benefits exceed the costs. The problem is that opinions vary about the magnitudes of these costs and benefits.

Alan J. Auerbach is a professor of economics at the University of Pennsylvania and a research associate of the National Bureau of Economic Research.

A role of economic research is to provide information that can improve the accuracy of such cost-benefit calculations. Toward this end, the National Bureau of Economic Research initiated a project on mergers and acquisitions to encourage research by leading academics on a variety of specific topics. The five papers that follow report on ongoing research being done in connection with this project. Although the project has not reached its conclusion, these papers taken together provide a general perspective on the recent corporate boom in mergers and acquisitions that is far less alarming than a casual inspection of the financial press would suggest.

Robert A. Taggart, Jr., explores the recent increase in junk bond financing and dispels a number of concerns that have been associated with this financial innovation. He shows that junk bonds represent a relatively small fraction of total corporate borrowing and a tiny fraction of the assets (about one-half of 1 percent) of the savings and loans insured by the FSLIC. The majority of junk bonds have not been issued in connection with merger or acquisition activity, and only a small fraction of such activity has been financed by junk bonds. Perhaps most important, he shows that junk bonds adjusted for risk have thus far performed favorably relative to higher-grade bonds. Taggart provides evidence that, overall, the use of junk bonds in takeovers has not significantly harmed the value of preexisting corporate liabilities.

The paper by Devra L. Golbe and Lawrence J. White shows that the current merger wave is far less important in magnitude than two such waves that occurred earlier in this century. They find there has been no noticeable impact on industrial or overall corporate concentration as a result of recent mergers and acquisitions.

Thus, the first two papers suggest that there is less cause for concern about the impact of mergers and acquisitions than some have argued. The third paper, by Richard S. Ruback, shows that various charter provisions enacted to resist takeovers have, on average, been injurious to company stockholders. In fact, they have induced a significant decline in the value of the firms' shares.

The reduction of federal income taxes is an important potential motive for two corporations to combine. The Tax Reform Act of 1986 includes provisions to reduce the tax benefits available from such activity. The research by Alan J. Auerbach and David Reishus suggests, however, that tax benefits were not a significant factor in the great majority of large mergers and acquisitions that occurred in the decade ending in 1983. Moreover, such mergers were not associated with increases in corporate leverage, suggesting that the tax deductibility of interest incurred in such takeovers was not a key factor in the aggregate, either.

One increasingly common type of transaction which may be an exception to this rule, for which interest deductibility could have played a more important role, is the leveraged buyout. Less information is available about such transactions by their nature (the businesses are going private), but Andrei Shleifer and Robert W. Vishny suggest that, tax considerations aside, these have been generally beneficial transactions to those concerned, generating a 50 percent increase in the value of initial shareholdings. In many cases the company that went public again increased its value many times over.

The questions addressed in these five papers have yet to be conclusively answered, and there are many other important questions that have not been asked. At the very least, however, this research demonstrates the value of gathering relevant information before forming judgments about the appropriate policy responses to the recent increase in the number of corporate mergers and acquisitions.

1 The Growth of the "Junk" Bond Market and Its Role in Financing Takeovers

Robert A. Taggart, Jr.

1.1 Introduction

"Junk" bonds, as they are popularly called, or "high-yield" bonds, as they are termed by those wishing to avoid pejorative connotations, are simply bonds that are either rated below investment grade or unrated altogether.[1] Fueled by the introduction of newly issued junk bonds in 1977, this segment of the bond market has grown rapidly in recent years and now accounts for more than 15 percent of public corporate bonds outstanding. However, the growth of junk bond financing, particularly in hostile takeover situations, has been bitterly denounced.

For example, Martin Lipton, a merger specialist with the firm of Wachtell, Lipton, Rosen, and Katz, has argued that junk bond financing threatens "the destruction of the fabric of American industry" (Williams 1984). In a similar vein, twelve U.S. senators signed a letter in support of Federal Reserve restrictions on junk bond–financed takeovers, that stated, "By substituting debt for equity on the balance sheets of the nation's corporations, junk bond financing drains financial resources from productive uses such as economic development and job creation" (Wynter 1985).

Robert A. Taggart, Jr., is a professor of finance in the School of Management, Boston University, and a research associate of the National Bureau of Economic Research.

Why did junk bond financing arise, and how important is its influence in the capital markets? Why has it been the target of such acrimony, and how justified are the charges of its critics? This paper seeks to answer these questions.

Section 1.2 describes the major forces that have shaped capital market developments generally in recent years. Against this backdrop, the growth and current dimensions of the junk bond market are traced in section 1.3. It is argued that junk bond financing is a natural outgrowth of the same forces that have influenced the capital market as a whole. Section 1.4 reviews both the charges that have been brought against junk bonds and the evidence available for assessing those charges, and section 1.5 offers conclusions.

1.2 Forces Underlying Recent Capital Market Developments

The past ten to fifteen years have been ones of highly uncertain inflation and interest rate volatility. Since the Federal Reserve announced in 1979 that it would pay less attention to interest rate levels, the standard deviations of returns on fixed income securities have more than doubled (Ibbotson 1985). Changing rates of inflation have contributed to sharp swings in the availability of internal funds relative to total corporate financing needs (Taggart 1986). Thus, U.S. corporations have had to move in and out of the external capital markets more frequently in recent years, and they have faced highly uncertain conditions when doing so.

In response to these conditions, corporations have placed greater emphasis on reducing the costs of raising external funds. They have gone further afield to tap new sources of funds, as is illustrated by the growth of Eurodollar bond financing by U.S. corporations from $300 million in 1975 to $20 billion in 1984 (Kidwell, Marr, and Thompson 1985). Even firms with little or no overseas operations, such as public utilities, have raised funds in this market. Corporations have also sought when possible to raise funds directly from investors, thus avoiding the administrative and regulatory costs implicit in borrowing from financial intermediaries. This is exemplified by the rapid growth of the commercial paper market, in which outstanding paper of nonfinancial corporations quadrupled to more than $80 billion between 1978 and 1985. As a result, commercial and industrial loans from large banks fell from 34 percent of nonfinancial business borrowing in 1978 to 28 percent in 1985.

Similarly, changes in investor behavior have been induced by more volatile conditions in capital markets. Investors have searched for higher-yielding securities after suffering losses from inflation, and they have been more inclined to trade securities in response to changing economic conditions. Annual secondary market trading volume in Treasury bonds, for example, has increased tenfold since 1978 to more than $10 trillion in 1985 (Frydl 1986). Among financial intermediaries, a similar desire for flexibility has manifested itself in the unbuckling of loan origination from investment, as in the growth of mortgage-backed securities.

Recent years have also witnessed increased competition among financial institutions. Making loans to prime customers has become more of a commodity-type business as U.S. banks have faced competition both from foreign banks and from the commercial paper market. Banks have thus turned increasingly to asset-based financing and other forms of lending to lower-grade credits in an attempt to maintain profit margins. A similar phenomenon has occurred in investment banking, where margins on underwriting bonds for large corporate customers have narrowed, especially since 1982, when the shelf registration rule (Rule 415) was adopted. This has in turn led to an emphasis on higher-margin activities, such as advising on mergers and acquisitions. Investment bankers have also tried to attract customers with innovative securities and transactions, such as zero coupon bonds and interest rate swaps.

Competitive upheaval has affected numerous other sectors of the U.S. economy as well. The effects of regulatory change, foreign competition, volatile commodity prices, and new technology have been felt in industries ranging from transportation and communication to energy and manufacturing. Mergers and divestitures, new investment, and plant closings have led to large capital flows into and out of these industries. In the financial markets, these activities have placed a premium on the ability to mobilize large amounts of capital quickly.

In the next section it will be argued that the growth of the junk bond market is a product of this same set of forces. It should also be noted that the turbulent economic environment resulting from these forces has given rise to a host of emotion-charged policy issues. These include the debate over "industrial policy," the soundness of corporate financial practices, the stability of financial intermediaries in the face of regulatory and competitive change, and the role of mergers and takeovers in economic growth. Since the growth of the junk bond market stems from the economic forces that gave rise to these issues, it should not be surprising that the market itself has become entwined in many of the same issues.

1.3   Dimensions of the Junk Bond Market

1.3.1   Growth of the Market

Prior to 1977, the public junk bond market consisted almost entirely of "fallen angels," or bonds whose initial investment grade ratings were subsequently lowered. As the first two columns of table 1.1 show, fallen angels accounted for about 5 percent, on average, of U.S. corporations' public straight debt outstanding between the beginning of 1970 and the end of 1976.

The market began to change in 1977, when bonds that were rated below investment grade from the start were first issued in significant quantities. Although Lehman Brothers is credited with having underwritten the first such issue (*Institutional Investor* 1985), Drexel Burnham Lambert turned this innovation into a major business thrust and quickly became the market leader.[2]

The economic conditions described in the preceding section were conducive to increased acceptance of junk bonds at this time. For example, investors' search for higher-yielding securities had already enhanced interest in lower-grade bonds, so new issues offered a way to satisfy this demand.

At the same time, the changing industrial structure was stimulating the growth of a number of medium-sized firms whose lack of credit history prevented them from qualifying for investment grade bond ratings. Junk bonds afforded such

Table 1.1   **Outstanding Debt of U.S. Corporations (billions of dollars)**

Year	Total Public Straight Bonds[a] (1)	Public Straight Junk Bonds[a] (2)	(2) as % of (1) (3)	Total Corporate Bonds[b] (4)	(2) as % of (4) (5)
1985	410.0	59.1	14.5	653.7	9.0
1984	371.1	41.7	11.2	568.9	7.3
1983	339.9	28.2	8.3	518.0	5.4
1982	320.9	18.5	5.8	487.4	3.8
1981	303.8	17.4	5.7	458.6	3.8
1980	282.0	15.1	5.4	431.7	3.5
1979	245.0	9.4	3.8	370.8	2.5
1978	245.0	9.4	3.8	370.8	2.5
1977	228.5	8.5	3.7	333.1	2.6
1976	209.9	8.0	3.8	304.4	2.6
1975	187.9	7.7	4.1	277.7	2.7
1974	167.0	11.1	6.6	251.9	4.4
1973	154.8	8.1	5.2	233.2	3.5
1972	145.7	7.1	4.9	219.1	3.2
1971	132.5	6.6	5.0	200.2	3.3
1970	116.2	7.0	6.0	176.5	4.0

[a]Measured as of June 30 for each year. Source: Altman and Nammacher (1985b, 1986).
[b]Average of beginning and ending years' figures. Source: Board of Governors of Federal Reserve System.

firms direct access to investors and thus provided a potentially lower-cost alternative to borrowing through financial intermediaries.

In investment banking, the competitive pressures described in the preceding section were already eroding the profitability of high-grade bond underwriting, so firms in the industry had become increasingly receptive to new market segments. Since only 6 percent of the roughly 11,000 public corporations in the United States qualify for investment grade ratings (Paulus 1986), junk bond underwriting appeared to offer a higher-margin business with potential for growth. Hence the development of the junk bond business in investment banking may be seen as analogous to commercial banks' pursuit of nonprime customers in an attempt to maintain profitability.

Newly issued junk bonds were an especially attractive business opportunity for Drexel Burnham, which had little established position in the higher-quality segment of bond underwriting and few competitive advantages on which it could build such a position. It did, however, have an established junk bond trading operation, which Michael Milken had been developing since the early 1970s. Drexel Burnham had already established a network of potential investors and the capability to serve as a secondary market–maker; together, these were key contributing factors to its dominance of junk bond underwriting. Issuers saw Drexel's investor network as giving it almost a unique ability to mobilize large amounts of capital quickly, while investors found junk bonds far more attractive when they could be resold in a liquid secondary market.[3]

It can be argued, in fact, that much of what was innovative about newly issued junk bonds was the ability to trade them. As Jensen (1986) has pointed out, junk bonds can be thought of as term loans that have been packaged to enhance their liquidity and divisibility. They are thus a substitute for bank loans and private placements, which the original lenders typically hold until maturity. In this light, the development of the junk bond market is analogous to the securitization process that has taken place in the mortgage market.

Table 1.2 documents the growth of the new issue portion of the junk bond market since 1977. Most new issues are unsecured public straight debt with typical maturities in the ten- to

Table 1.2	Yearly Public Issues of Corporate Debt (billions of dollars)		
Year	Total Public Bond Issues by U.S. Corporations[a] (1)	Public Issues of Straight Junk Bonds[b] (2)	(2) as % of (1) (3)
1986 (1st half)	114.3	15.8	13.8
1985	120.0	19.8	16.5
1984	73.6	15.8	21.4
1983	47.6	8.5	17.8
1982	44.3	3.2	7.2
1981	38.1	1.7	4.6
1980	41.6	2.1	5.0
1979	25.8	1.7	6.5
1978	19.8	2.1	10.8
1977	24.1	1.1	4.6

[a]1986 figure from *Investment Dealer's Digest*. Figures for 1977–85 from *Federal Reserve Bulletin*.

[b]1986 figure from *Investment Dealer's Digest*. Figures for 1977–85 from Drexel Burnham Lambert (1986).

fifteen-year range.[4] Since 1983, junk bonds of this type have averaged nearly 17 percent of total (convertible plus straight) public bond issues by U.S. corporations. Largely as a result of the increase in new issues, the share of junk bonds in total corporate bonds outstanding has also grown substantially. The market's rapid growth, in fact, is reflected in the continually increasing estimates of its size. According to a Morgan Stanley estimate (Altman and Nammacher 1986) shown in table 1.1, straight public junk bonds outstanding amounted to $59.1 billion in mid-1985. This represents over 14 percent of straight public corporate debt and 9 percent of total corporate bonds outstanding. Drexel Burnham (1986) provides an estimate of $82 billion in junk bonds by year-end 1985, which represents 19.1 percent of year-end public straight debt and nearly 12 percent of total corporate bonds outstanding at the end of the year. When convertibles and private placements with registration rights are also included, the share of junk bonds is slightly higher.[5] Finally, Morgan Stanley's data indicate that, as a result of both new issues and bond downgrades, public junk bonds outstanding had grown to $92.9 billion by June 30, 1986.

1.3.2 Investors

Financial institutions are the primary investors in junk bonds; Drexel Burnham estimates their total holdings to be between 80 and 90 percent. This represents between $45 and $84 billion in total holdings, depending on the date on which total junk bonds outstanding are estimated. Within the financial institutions category, approximately $5.5 billion (or 7 percent of outstanding junk bonds) was held by savings and loan associations, including their unconsolidated but wholly owned subsidiaries at year-end 1985.[6] There were also forty high-yield bond mutual funds by the end of 1985, with total assets of approximately $12 billion (about 15 percent of outstanding junk bonds). This had grown to forty-five funds with nearly $21 billion in assets by mid-1986. However, the assets of these funds were not invested exclusively in junk bonds (Altman and Nammacher 1985b, 1986). Other institutional holders of junk bonds include pension funds, insurance companies, commercial banks, and investment banking firms.

1.3.3 Junk Bond Returns and Risk

As one would expect, junk bonds experience more defaults than investment grade bonds, but as a group, they also tend to have higher returns. For the period 1974–85, the annual default rate on rated junk bonds averaged 1.53 percent, compared with 0.09 percent for all rated public straight bonds (Altman and Nammacher 1986).[7] During 1985 the default rate for junk bonds (1.68 percent) was slightly higher than its previous average, but at the same time the default rate for all bonds (0.23 percent) was substantially higher than average. For the first six months of 1986, the rate for junk bonds increased again to about 3 percent.

Although differences in returns are sensitive to the period chosen, junk bond returns have generally compared favorably with those of higher-grade bonds. For the period 1978–85, for example, Altman and Nammacher (1986) calculated a compound annual rate of return of 12.4 percent for junk bonds compared with 9.7 percent for the Shearson Lehman Long-Term Government Bond Index. For the period 1976–85, the average total reinvested return for high-yield mutual funds was 206.8 percent, compared with 178.0 percent for U.S. government bond funds. Using internal worksheets from market-makers, Blume and Keim (1984) constructed their own index of junk bond returns and found an annualized compound monthly rate of return of 20.3 percent for the period January 1982 to May 1984, compared with 15.0 percent for a portfolio of AAA-rated bonds. For the same period, they also found a positive (though not quite statistically significant) "alpha," or risk-adjusted excess rate of return of 0.61 percent, compared with 0.24 percent for AAA bonds.[8] It would be unjustified, of course, to extrapolate any of these specific return spreads to future periods, but there is substantial evidence that portfolios of junk bonds have performed relatively well in the recent past.

1.3.4 Junk Bonds and Merger Activity

By far the most controversial use of junk bonds has been in leveraged buyouts and takeovers. Drexel Burnham began selling junk bonds to finance leveraged buyouts in 1981, and in 1983 the firm conceived the idea of using junk bond financing commitments in connection with hostile takeovers. Again, Drexel's trading capability and investor network, which gave it the ability to raise large amounts of funds on relatively short notice, made acquisition activity a natural extension of its existing business. In particular, it had already established trading relationships with a number of so-called corporate raiders, including the Belzberg family, Carl Lindner, and Saul Steinberg (Bianco 1985).

Although a variety of financing structures have been used, the one attracting the most attention was that in which a potential acquirer, backed by financing commitments from investors, makes a tender offer for some fraction of the target company's shares. The commitments represent the investors' promise to purchase some amount of junk bonds or other securities, provided that the specified fraction of shares is tendered under the terms of the offer. The securities may be issued through a shell corporation, set up specifically for the purpose of acquiring the target's shares, but they are not explicitly collateralized by those shares. If the tender offer succeeds, the target company's assets can then be used as collateral for any additional loans needed to complete the acquisition. Whether or not the offer succeeds, the investors receive commitment fees ranging from 3/8 percent to 1 percent of the funds committed (Bleakley 1985).

From the acquirer's standpoint, the principal advantage of this structure is speed. Delays are felt to favor the target company in a hostile takeover attempt, and except for large acquirers, raising the needed funds can often be a source of delay. By relying on its established investor network, however, Drexel Burnham found that it could obtain sizable financing commitments in a relatively short period. This in turn considerably enhanced the ability of an acquirer to attempt the takeover even of a much larger target. Of course, investors' willingness to make these commitments on short notice depended on a good relationship with Drexel Burnham, based on successful investments in previous dealings with the firm. As long as this relationship could be maintained, though, Drexel Burnham was able to raise capital quickly.

Not surprisingly, the increased ability of "raiders" to attempt the takeover of even very large companies aroused anger and suspicion in a number of quarters, and several bills were introduced in Congress aimed at curbing junk bond financing of takeovers. Some critics were especially disturbed that a small number of large investors appeared to be taking turns financing one another in takeover raids.[9]

To date, however, the only legislative or regulatory action taken against junk bonds has been by the Federal Reserve Board. Despite the fact that junk bonds issued in takeovers are not explicitly collateralized by the shares of the target company, the Fed voted in January 1986 to apply margin regulations to stock purchases by shell corporations. The ruling stipulated numerous exceptions, however, and thus made it clear that it was aimed directly at hostile takeovers using the shell financing structure just described.[10]

While it is clear that junk bonds have sparked heated controversy, it is less clear how important their actual role in financing acquisitions has been. Estimates of the amount of junk bond financing used in acquisitions differ widely but a range of possibilities can be established.

Drexel Burnham (1985), for example, estimates that in 1984, about $1.7 billion in publicly issued junk bonds was associated with acquisitions and leveraged buyouts. This represents about 11 percent of total public junk bond issues for the year and about 1.4 percent of the total 1984 value of merger and acquisition activity.[11] Of this amount, Drexel Burnham estimates that $0.6 billion, or 4 percent of 1984's total public junk bond issues, was associated with hostile takeovers. A very preliminary Drexel Burnham estimate (reported in Jensen 1986) indicates that during 1985, junk bond acquisition financing may have risen to $3.8 billion, which represents 19 percent of total public junk bond issues for the year and 2.7 percent of total merger financing.

The Federal Reserve Board, by contrast, estimates that $6.5 billion, or 41 percent of 1984's total junk bond issues, was related to mergers or acquisitions in some way (Martin 1985). In addition, it estimates that $4.3 billion in privately placed junk bonds was merger related, so that $10.8 billion in all, or about 9 percent of 1984's total merger and acquisition activity, was financed with junk bonds.[12]

Finally, Morgan Stanley gives an intermediate figure, estimating that junk bond financing of acquisitions and leveraged buyouts came to about $3.3 billion in 1984 and $6.2 billion in 1985 (Paulus 1986). This represents 21 percent and 31 percent, respectively, of total junk bond issues for those years. It also represents 2.6 percent and 4.5 percent, respectively, of the total value of merger activity for 1984 and 1985.

1.3.5 Conclusions about the Size of the Market

The inconsistencies in the figures cited above make it clear that the dimensions of the junk bond market are hard to determine precisely. Nevertheless, some general conclusions seem warranted.

First, the growth of the market has been impressive. Particularly since 1982, the share of junk bonds in both new issues and total corporate bonds outstanding has increased sharply. There can be no doubt that junk bonds now represent an important segment of the corporate bond market.

Second, while the importance of junk bonds must be conceded, it should also be recognized that they hardly threaten to overwhelm the market. The data in table 1.2, for example, do not give strong grounds for predicting that junk bonds' market share will experience further rapid increases in the immediate future.

Third, the role of junk bond financing in mergers and acquisitions must likewise be seen as significant, but not predominant. By any set of estimates, only a small part of the value of junk bonds issued is used for acquisitions. The rest is used to finance ongoing business operations. In addition, merger-related junk bond issues represent only a small fraction of total merger and acquisition activity.

1.4 Policy Issues Surrounding the Junk Bond Market

It has been argued in preceding sections that uncertain inflation and interest rate volatility, increased competition in the financial services industry, and the process of corporate restructuring have all contributed to the growth of the junk bond market. These forces have also produced a turbulent economic environment, which has spurred policy debates about the level of debt in the economy, the stability of financial institutions, and the fairness and efficiency of the corporate takeover process. It is not surprising that the growth of the junk bond market, a product of the same economic forces, has been accompanied by the same policy debates. However, just as it would be implausible to argue that the junk bond market has itself been a root cause of interest rate volatility, financial services competition, and corporate restructuring, it would be equally implausible to argue that junk bonds have been fundamentally responsible for the perceived ills described in these policy debates. Let us consider several of these policy issues in turn.

1.4.1   Is There Too Much Debt in the U.S. Financial System?

There may be. If there is, however, it would be difficult to argue that the corporate sector is primarily responsible. It is true that there has been a fairly steady increase in recent years in corporate debt-equity ratios measured in book value terms. When measured in market value terms, by contrast, adjusting for inflation and for changes in the perceived ability of assets to generate cash, the debt-equity ratio has decreased substantially since 1974. In 1985, for example, the estimated market value debt-equity ratio for U.S. corporations was .37, compared with .61 in 1974 and an average of .46 for the period 1975–84.[13]

Moreover, as indicated in table 1.1, junk bonds do not account for a major fraction of total corporate debt. Since at least some portion of newly issued junk bonds are presumably a substitute for bank borrowing or private placements that corporations would otherwise have made, it is especially hard to argue that junk bonds have exerted any substantial upward influence on the overall corporate debt-equity ratio. Fears about the overall level of debt have been used to rationalize restrictions on the use of junk bonds in takeovers (Schultz 1985), such as the imposition of margin regulations by the Federal Reserve Board. Since takeovers account for only a small fraction of even total junk bond financing, such restrictions could hardly have much effect on total corporate debt.

1.4.2   Does Merger Activity Contribute to Increased Corporate Debt?

Available evidence indicates that this is not the case. A study by Becketti (1986), for example, found no statistical linkage between the value of merger activity in immediately preceding years and the total current level of domestic non-financial debt. But even if one disputes this evidence, the amount of junk bond merger financing is so small relative to total merger activity, as indicated in section 1.3.5, that junk bonds could not have made much of a contribution to any merger-induced increase in total debt.

1.4.3   Are Takeovers and Their Associated Tactics Harmful to the Economy?

This question has been widely debated, and a complete discussion is clearly beyond the scope of this paper. The point is, though, that this issue is also far beyond the scope of the junk bond market. Corporate raiders, greenmail and break-up acquisitions, or "asset-stripping," have all been blamed to some degree on junk bond financing.[14] But while it is true that junk bond financing has facilitated hostile takeover bids by enabling potential acquirers to raise capital quickly, hostile takeovers existed long before the introduction of junk bond financing and would continue to exist even if the junk bond market were heavily curtailed by regulation or legislation. Moreover, there would appear to be no more compelling reasons to pay greenmail to a junk bond financed raider than to a raider financed by some other means. In the same vein, breaking up assets makes economic sense only when they are perceived to be worth more separately than together, whether or not the assets have been financed with junk bonds.

1.4.4   Do Junk Bond Holdings by Financial Institutions Pose a Threat to the Deposit Insurance Agencies?

The fear here is that savings and loans, in particular, have abused their new diversification power by purchasing exceptionally risky assets. In so doing, it is charged, they have shifted risk to the Federal Savings and Loan Insurance Corporation.

In the broadest sense, this fear does not appear to be warranted. Federally chartered S&Ls are currently allowed to hold 1 percent of their assets in unrated bonds. Their 10 percent commercial lending authority may also be used to purchase junk bonds, giving total allowed holdings of 11 percent. State-chartered S&Ls in some states may devote larger fractions of their assets to junk bonds. In the aggregate, however, the Federal Home Loan Bank Board estimates the S&Ls held, on average, a total of $5.5 billion in junk bonds during 1985.[15] This represents approximately one-half of 1 percent of the total assets of FSLIC-insured institutions, and thus junk bonds would not appear to pose a system-wide threat to the FSLIC.

Nevertheless, it is true that junk bond holdings are very concentrated among the nation's S&Ls. For example, as of June 1985, ten S&Ls (out of 3,180 FSLIC-insured institutions) held $4.64 billion in junk bonds. This accounts for 77 percent of total junk bond holdings by S&Ls during that month and represents about 10 percent of total assets by those ten institutions. Five of these institutions are located in California and three in Texas, states that have more liberal asset composition regulations for state-chartered S&Ls. Furthermore, a single institution, Columbia Saving and Loan Association of Beverly Hills, California, held approximately $1 billion in junk bonds at this time, and by June 30, 1986, it had increased its junk bond holdings to $2.3 billion, or 28 percent of its total assets (Hilder 1986).

It is possible, then, that junk bonds could pose a problem for the FSLIC, albeit a problem confined to a relatively small number of institutions. But as in the debates discussed above, the issue is really much broader than the junk bond market itself. There is a host of risky financial practices in which S&Ls or other depository institutions might engage. It has yet to be demonstrated that junk bonds are significantly riskier than many other investments, such as construction loans or financial futures positions, and junk bond losses have not been a contributing factor in S&L failures to date. The FSLIC may indeed need to improve its procedures for monitoring and assessing S&L risk and for pricing deposit insurance, but junk bonds appear to be a small part of this overall problem.

1.4.5   Does Junk Bond Issuance Harm Other Bondholders?

The corporate restructuring phenomenon has increased leverage for a number of firms. This has come about through mergers, leveraged buyouts, and stock repurchases. In addition, many firms have altered the overall riskiness of their assets through acquisitions and divestitures. As a result of such transactions, the outstanding debt of a number of firms has been downgraded, and bondholders have suffered losses.[16] To the extent that newly issued junk bonds have been involved in restructuring transactions, they have shared some of the blame for these losses and some see the problem of bondholder expropriation as an important legal issue (McDaniel 1986).

There is little reason to suppose, though, that transferring wealth from bondholders is a primary motivation for issuing junk bonds. Firms could not impose extensive damage on existing bondholders without severely penalizing the terms on which they could raise funds in the future. Empirical studies also suggest that, while restructuring transactions are beneficial to shareholders, they do not, on average, cause significant losses for bondholders.[17]

There can be no doubt, of course, that bondholders have experienced significant losses in individual cases.[18] The restructuring phenomenon reflects a period of upheaval that was not widely anticipated, either by management or investors, at the time many outstanding bonds were issued. Thus, in retrospect, some investors have found themselves inadequately protected. In response, both investors and management have sought new protective mechanisms so as to make future bond issues more attractive. Several issues of "poison put" bonds have been made, for example, which allow holders to turn in their bonds for cash or stock in the event of a change in control of the issuing company (Hertzberg 1986). Similar provisions in some recent private placements allow loans to be called if a major restructuring occurs (Picker 1986). While restructuring transactions may pose difficult problems of negotiation between bondholders and firms, however, it is not clear that additional legislative or regulatory action is called for.

1.5 Conclusion

This paper has attempted to assess the size and influence of the junk bond market. Newly issued junk bonds represent a significant financial innovation. Spawned by the forces of interest rate volatility, competition in financial services, and industrial restructuring, they have tapped a significant pocket of investor demand, thereby allowing many corporations to raise funds more quickly and on better terms than would otherwise have been available.

At the same time, the significance that junk bonds have been accorded in policy debates appears to stem more from their symbolic value than their real influence. The mere mention of their label can conjure up visions of corporate raiders and heavy debt burdens. But regardless of one's position on the larger policy issues, actions directed at the junk bond market by itself seem unlikely to have a radical impact on the aggregate level of debt, the amount of corporate restructuring activity, or the safety of the financial system.

Notes

I am grateful to Richard Pickering of the Federal Home Loan Bank Board's Office of Policy and Economic Research, Eric H. Siber of Drexel Burnham Lambert, Inc., and Richard S. Wilson of Merrill Lynch Capital Markets for providing helpful information. They bear no responsibility, however, for any errors this paper may contain.

1.   Under Moody's rating system, therefore, junk bonds are those rated Ba or lower, while under Standard & Poor's, they are defined as BB or lower. For ease of expression, the more common term, "junk" bonds, will be used throughout the paper, but no derogatory implications are intended by that usage.

2.   Drexel Burnham's dominance is illustrated by the fact that it served as lead manager for 56 percent of the value of total public junk bond issues during the period 1978–85 (Altman and Nammacher 1986).

3.   Secondary trading volume in junk bonds is apparently substantial relative to other types of corporate bonds. G. Chris Anderson of Drexel Burnham has estimated that annual secondary market trading volume currently amounts to $240 billion (Reich 1986). This is about 20 percent of the annual dollar trading volume for New York Stock Exchange stocks.

4.   The average years to maturity (ignoring sinking funds) of new junk bond issues fell from nineteen years in 1978 to eleven years in 1985 (Altman and Nammacher 1986). Call and sinking fund provisions are usually similar

to those found on other corporate bonds, although very recently a few junk bond issues have contained "net worth" clauses, stipulating that some or all of the issue must be called at par if the issuer's net worth falls below a certain level. In general, however, junk bonds tend to carry fewer restrictive covenants than investment grade bonds.

5.   Private placements with registration rights are issues that are initially privately placed, but that give the original investors the right to have the issue registered for public trading at some future point. Such issues might be used, for example, in situations in which a need to raise funds quickly favors a private placement, but in which the initial investor would ultimately like to be able to trade his bonds in the public market.

6.   This information was provided by the Federal Home Loan Bank Board's Office of Policy and Economic Research. The implications of S&L holdings of junk bonds will be discussed further in section 1.4.

7.   The default rate is measured as the par value of bonds of a given type that default during a year, divided by the par value of total outstanding bonds of that type for the year. Since investors do not lose the entire par value of their investment in a default, it should be noted that this rate may considerably overstate actual investor losses.

8.   Perhaps surprisingly, Blume and Keim also found a lower monthly standard deviation of returns (2.74 percent) for junk bonds during this period than for AAA bonds (3.59 percent). It should be noted, however, that the characteristics (call provisions, duration, etc.) of the two samples were not matched and that this was a relatively short period.

9.   For example, Bleakley (1985) reports that of $3.1 billion in junk bond financing commitments for five takeover attempts (three of which were ultimately successful) during 1984 and 1985, $1.2 billion in commitments came from just eight investors. Moreover, four of the eight (the Belzberg family, Nelson Peltz of Triangle Industries, Saul Steinberg of Reliance Group, and Stephen Wynn of Golden Nugget), who together made $643 million in commitments, were themselves regarded as raiders.

10.   Specifically, the Fed stated that margin rules would not apply under any of the following conditions: (1) the acquiring company has substantial assets or cash flow apart from the shares of the target; (2) the parent company guarantees the debt of the shell acquisition corporation; (3) there is a merger agreement between the acquirer and the target; (4) debt securities are offered to the public; (5) financing commitments are contingent on the shell corporation's acquisition of sufficient shares to complete a merger, under state laws, without the approval of the target's shareholders or directors (Langley and Williams 1986).

11.   Figures on total merger activity are taken from the May-June 1986 issue of *Mergers and Acquisitions* magazine.

12.   The Congressional Research Service (Winch and Brancato 1985) estimates that about $1.7 billion in junk bond financing was associated with leveraged buyouts during 1984. This also represents about 9 percent of the total 1984 value of leveraged buyouts.

13.   These figures were estimated using the technique described in Taggart (1985). The Federal Reserve Board, using a different technique, has produced estimates that are numerically higher (Martin 1985). However, the same qualitative conclusions about the debt-equity ratio's pattern over time continue to hold.

14.   As an example of the latter, Rohatyn (1985) asserts, "Whether large corporations can be treated like artichokes and simply torn apart without any regard for employees, communities, or customers solely in order to pay off speculative debt is a further question for public policy."

15.   This figure includes junk bonds held by unconsolidated but wholly owned S&L subsidiaries, so it exaggerates somewhat the junk bond holdings of S&L parent companies.

16.   For example, Moody's downgraded corporate bonds having a total par value of $107.5 billion during 1985, or about 16 percent of the total par value of corporate bonds outstanding. Bonds having a par value of $40.8 billion, or 38 percent of the value of downgrades, were downgraded as a result of restructuring transactions (Goldberg 1986).

17.   Studies of this issue include Dann (1981) on stock repurchases, Dennis and McConnell (1986) on mergers, and Hite and Owers (1983) and Schipper and Smith (1983) on spin-offs. A study of the formation of captive finance subsidiaries by Kim, McConnell, and Greenwood (1977) did present some evidence of significant bondholder losses but a more recent study of the same phenomenon by Malitz (1986) does not confirm that finding. None of these studies, however, include the most recent round of corporate restructuring transactions.

18.   For evidence of such losses see Alexander, Benson, and Gunderson (1986) and Wansley and Fayez (1986).

References

Alexander, G. J., P. G. Benson, and E. W. Gunderson. 1986. "Asset Redeployment: Trans World Corporation's Spinoff of TWA." *Financial Management* 15 (Summer): 50–58.

Altman, E. I., and S. A. Nammacher. 1985a. *The Default Rate Experience on High-Yield Corporate Debt.* New York: Morgan Stanley & Co., March.

————. 1985b. *The Anatomy of the High-Yield Debt Market.* New York: Morgan Stanley & Co., September.

————. 1986. *The Anatomy of the High-Yield Debt Market: 1985 Update.* New York: Morgan Stanley & Co., June.

Anderson, G. C. 1985. Testimony before the Subcommittee on Domestic Monetary Policy. House Committee on Banking, Finance, and Urban Affairs. Hearings on the Financing of Mergers and Acquisitions, May 3.

Becketti, S. 1986. "Corporate Mergers and the Business Cycle: Federal Reserve Bank of Kansas City." *Economic Reviews* 71 (May): 13–26.

Bianco, A. 1985. "How Drexel's Wunderkind Bankrolls the Raiders." *Business Week* (March 4).

Bleakley, F. R. 1985. "The Power and the Perils of Junk Bonds." *New York Times* (April 14).

Blume, M. E., and D. B. Keim. 1984. "Risk and Return Characteristics of Lower-Grade Bonds." Working paper, Rodney White Center for Financial Research, the Wharton School, December.

Carney, W. 1985. "Junk Bonds Don't Merit a Black-Hat Image." *The Wall Street Journal* (April 29).

Dann, L. Y. 1981. "Common Stock Repurchases: An Analysis of Returns to Bondholders and Stockholders." *Journal of Financial Economics* 9 (June): 113–38.

Dennis, D. K., and J. J. McConnell. 1986. "Corporate Mergers and Security Returns." *Journal of Financial Economics* 16 (June): 143–87.

Drexel Burnham Lambert, Inc. 1985. *Financing America's Growth: High Yield-Bonds* (April).

―――――. 1986. *The Case for High-Yield Securities* (April).

Ehrbar, A. 1985. "Have Takeovers Gone Too Far?" *Fortune* (May 27).

Frydl, E. J. 1986. "The Challenge of Financial Change." *Seventy-First Annual Report*. Federal Reserve Bank of New York.

Goldberg, H. H. 1986. "Corporate Bond Market Outlook 1986." *Moody's Bond Survey* 78 (February).

Hertzberg, D. 1986. "'Poison-Put' Bonds Are Latest Weapon in Companies' Anti-Takeover Strategy." *The Wall Street Journal* (February 13).

Hilder, D. B. 1986. "Bank Board Staff Expects to Offer Rules Curbing Thrifts' 'Junk Bond' Investments." *The Wall Street Journal* (September 28).

Hite, G. L., and J. E. Owers. 1983. "Security Price Reactions Around Corporate Spin-Off Announcements." *Journal of Financial Economics* 12 (December): 409–36.

Hughes, K. A. 1985. "Columbia Savings' Chief, Spiegel, Invests $1 Billion of S&L's Assets in 'Junk Bonds.'" *The Wall Street Journal* (June 7).

Ibbotson Associates, R. G., Inc. 1985. *Stocks, Bonds, Bills, and Inflation, 1985 Yearbook*. Chicago.

Institutional Investor. 1985. "Banker of the Year." August.

Jensen, M. C. 1986. "The Takeover Controversy: Analysis and Evidence." Working paper, Harvard Business School, July.

Joseph, F. H. 1985. "High-Yield Bonds Aren't 'Junk.'" *The Wall Street Journal* (May 31).

Kidwell, D. S., M. W. Marr, and G. R. Thompson. 1985. "Eurodollar Bonds: Alternative Financing for U.S. Companies." *Financial Management* 14 (Winter): 18–27.

Kim, E. H., J. J. McConnell, and P. Greenwood. 1977. "Capital Structure Rearrangement and Me-First Rules in an Efficient Capital Market." *Journal of Finance* 32 (June): 789–810.

Langley, M., and J. D. Williams, 1986. "Fed Board Votes 3–2 to Restrict the Use of 'Junk' Bonds in Corporate Takeovers." *The Wall Street Journal* (January 9).

McDaniel, M. W. 1986. "Bondholders and Corporate Governance." *Business Lawyer* 41 (February): 413–60.

Malitz, I. B. 1986. "Do Owners Deliberately Expropriate Bondholder Wealth? The Case of Captive Finance Subsidiaries." Working paper, University of Illinois at Chicago, May.

Martin, P. 1985. Testimony before the Subcommittee on Domestic Monetary Policy. House Committee on Banking, Finance, and Urban Affairs, Hearings on the Financing of Mergers and Acquisitions, May 3.

Paulus, J. D. 1986. "Corporate Restructuring, 'Junk,' and Leverage: Too Much or Too Little?" *Economic Perspectives*. New York: Morgan Stanley & Co., March 12.

Picker, I. 1986. "Takeover Defenses Enter the Private Market." *Investment Dealer's Digest* (April 14).

Reich, C. 1986. "Milken the Magnificent." *Institutional Investor* 20 (August): 81–97.

Rohatyn, F. G. 1985. "Junk Bonds and Other Securities Swill." *The Wall Street Journal* (April 18).

Schipper, K., and A. Smith. 1983. "Effects of Recontracting on Shareholder Wealth: The Case of Voluntary Spin-Offs." *Journal of Financial Economics* 12 (December): 437–67.

Schultz, F. 1985. "The Fed's Vain Limit on Takeover Debt." *The Wall Street Journal* (December 23).

Stewart, J. B., and R. L. Rundle. 1985. "Drexel Burnham Mulls a Future Threatened by Junk-Bond Curbs." *The Wall Street Journal* (December 13).

Taggart, R. A., Jr. 1985. "Secular Patterns in the Financing of U.S. Corporations." In B. M. Friedman, ed., *Corporate Capital Structures in the United States*. Chicago: University of Chicago Press.

———. 1986. "Have U.S. Corporations Grown Financially Weak?" In B . M. Friedman, ed., *Financing Corporate Capital Formation*. Chicago: University of Chicago Press.

Wansley, J. W., and E. Fayez. 1986. "Stock Repurchases and Securityholders' Returns: A Case Study of Teledyne." *Journal of Financial Research* 9 (Summer): 179–91.

Williams, J. D. 1984. "How 'Junk Financings' Aid Corporate Raiders in Hostile Acquisitions." *The Wall Street Journal* (December 6).

Winch, K. F., and C. K. Brancato. 1985. *The Role of High-Yield Bonds (Junk Bonds) in Capital Markets and Corporate Takeovers: Public Policy Implications*. Congressional Research Service, Library of Congress, April 20.

Wynter, L. E. 1985. "U.S. Agencies, SEC Object to Fed Plan to Curb Junk Bonds Used in Takeovers." *The Wall Street Journal* (December 24).

2 Mergers and Acquisitions in the U.S. Economy: An Aggregate and Historical Overview

Devra L. Golbe and Lawrence J. White

2.1 Introduction

Mergers and acquisitions in the U.S. economy of the 1980s continue to attract a considerable amount of popular, professional, and political attention. Periodic announcements of mergers between large firms (General Electric and RCA), of hostile tender offers (Mesa and Unocal), and of leveraged buyouts (Beatrice) command the media's attention and comment. The entities are large, the announcements are frequent, and the changes can be unsettling, at least to some.

These changes in corporate ownership and structure need to be placed in a proper historical and analytical perspective. The American economy appears to have experienced major merger waves in earlier eras; the 1980s are not the first such period. A better comprehension of the basic forces motivating mergers and acquisitions may help us understand why they occur more frequently at some times than others. Are these events random, or are there systematic relationships that provide explanations for the patterns that are observed?

This paper is both aggregative and historical in approach. That is, we will not be focusing on individual mergers or on

Devra L. Golbe is an associate professor of economics at Hunter College of the City University of New York.

Lawrence J. White is a board member of the Federal Home Loan Board and a professor of economics at the Graduate School of Business Administration, New York University.

cross-section studies of such mergers.[1] Instead, we will focus on aggregate numbers (and, where possible, values) of mergers and acquisitions during relatively short time periods (a three-month quarter or a year) and examine the historical patterns of these aggregates. This approach has been (surprisingly, at least to us) relatively neglected,[2] but it should put short-run events in better perspective and provide a useful supplement to the cross-section studies.

The remainder of the paper is organized as follows: Section 2.2 briefly describes the data that are publicly available for conducting historical analyses and their drawbacks and presents the historical patterns that can be constructed from these data. In section 2.3, we turn to the analytical underpinnings of the merger and acquisition process, and we develop hypotheses that can be tested empirically. In section 2.4 we present the preliminary empirical results of this testing. Section 2.5 offers our conclusions.

2.2   The Data, Their Drawbacks, and Some Historical Patterns

2.2.1   The Data and Their Drawbacks

To obtain a suitable historical perspective on the current wave of mergers and acquisitions, one needs a long, comprehensive, consistent set of data on mergers and their likely determinants. Unfortunately, no such data series on mergers exists, and we must compromise. Indeed, the data problems are sufficiently important that we believe a detailed discussion of the data is necessary.

One data problem is especially pervasive and warrants preliminary discussion. No data series includes *every* merger and acquisition in the economy; all series have a lower limit on dollar size of transactions that are included. For example, one data series discussed below includes only those mergers in which the acquired firm had assets of $10 million or more. This kind of limitation poses two problems. First, it means that smaller transactions are not recorded. If these smaller transactions tend to follow the same pattern as larger transactions, or if they are, in aggregate, relatively unimportant, than little has been lost. Otherwise, the series may be providing a misleading picture, and since the transactions below the lower limit are not recorded, there is no way to tell.

Second, if the period covered by the time series was one of significant inflation, then the fixed dollar lower limit will artificially increase the number of recorded transactions over time. In essence, the pattern of rising prices through the time period covered by the series will mean that some transactions of a given real size would fall below the fixed cutoff point in the early years and hence not be recorded. In later years, inflation would drive the nominal value of the same transactions above the cutoff point, so that they would be recorded. The longer the time period covered by a series and the greater the inflation, the more substantial is the problem of a spurious increase in the number of recorded transactions.

Our discussion will first focus on the data available for the period after World War II and then discuss the data for the prewar period.

Post–World War II

There are three basic sources of time-series data on mergers and acquisitions for the postwar period: the U.S. Federal Trade Commission (FTC), the periodical *Mergers and Acquisitions,* and the annual reports of W. T. Grimm & Co. We will discuss each of these sources, the nature of the data, and their strengths and drawbacks, in turn.

U.S. FTC. The FTC collected and published data on mergers in the manufacturing and mining sectors of the U.S. economy for the years 1948–79.[3] One basic data set covered all mergers in which the acquired firm was in the manufacturing or mining sectors, had at least $10 million in assets (book value), and for which information on the acquisition was publicly available.[4] The FTC published annual figures for both the numbers of mergers and the book value of the assets acquired. It also provided the relevant information on each transaction, so that quarterly series on numbers of mergers and their value could be constructed.

A second FTC series also covered the manufacturing and mining sectors, with annual numbers of merger transactions extending from 1940 through 1979 and quarterly numbers extending from 1940 through 1954.[5] This second series appears to have been more inclusive than the first, since a far larger number of transactions are registered. But unfortunately, the FTC did not indicate the inclusion criteria for this series.

The FTC data have a number of shortcomings: First, they cover only the manufacturing and mining sectors, which declined substantially in relative importance during the 1948–79 period and currently constitute only a quarter of U.S. GNP. Second, the $10 million lower limit clearly created distortions, since the general price level (as measured by the GNP deflator) tripled over the thirty-two years covered by the data. Third, the series excluded acquisitions by an individual or groups of individuals and hence would appear to exclude most leveraged buyouts of divisions or of whole companies. Fourth, the FTC ceased collecting and publishing these data in 1981 (with 1979 as the last year for which data were made available), so the series does not cover the merger wave of the 1980s.

The periodical Mergers and Acquisitions. The quarterly issues of the periodical *Mergers and Acquisitions* (*M&A*) list the number of mergers and acquisitions consummated in recent quarters for the entire U.S. economy. Prior to the fourth quarter of 1980, the lower limit for inclusion in the series was a purchase price of at least $700,000; in that quarter the lower limit was raised to $1,000,000. A quarterly series on domestic companies being purchased (either by domestic or foreign companies) extends from the first quarter of 1967 to the present. A series that also includes domestic companies' purchases of foreign companies extends from the fourth quarter of 1972 to the present. Both series include leveraged buyouts.

The *M&A* series have a number of drawbacks. First, they do not extend as far back as the FTC series. Second, the lower limit for inclusion changed abruptly in the middle of the series and, even so, does not properly adjust for the tripling of prices that occurred during the period covered. Third, integrating or splicing the *M&A* series with the FTC series (so as to create a longer overall series that would be up-to-date) cannot be done easily or automatically, since the series cover different universes and have different criteria for inclusion.

W. T. Grimm & Co. W. T. Grimm & Co. publishes data on the number of merger and acquisition announcements in the entire U.S. economy. Their published annual series extends from 1963 through the present; their quarterly series extends from the first quarter of 1974 through the present. The lower limit for inclusion is a transaction involving at least a $500,000 purchase price.

The Grimm data have the same problems as the *M&A* data: a limited historical reach, fixed lower limit for inclusion, and difficulties of integration with the FTC data. Also, the Grimm data pertain to announcements rather than completions.

Pre–World War II

The major source of merger data for the period 1895–1920 is the study conducted by Ralph Nelson.[6] Nelson's data appear to cover only the manufacturing and mining sectors. The cutoff limits are not explicit; rather, Nelson relies on financial reporting during the period covered. Nelson provides annual and quarterly series[7] for the number of transactions and the book value of the acquired firms.[8]

For the period 1919–39, Willard Thorpe compiled a quarterly series on the number of mergers in the manufacturing and mining sectors, which is reproduced by Nelson.[9] The criteria for inclusion are unclear. The Thorpe series was continued in 1940 by the broad FTC series discussed in the text above, and the two series appear to be consistent and compatible.

In sum, while data series that include the recent history of mergers and acquisitions exist, they do not extend back far enough to provide adequate historical perspective. The FTC data do provide sufficient historical reach, but they end in 1979. Further, they exclude the service sector, an increasingly important part of our economy. The inconsistencies of the more recent data series with the FTC data complicate statistical inference. In the next section, we provide some graphical representations of the historical patterns in mergers and acquisitions.

2.2.2   Some Historical Patterns

Having described the data series and their drawbacks, we now present a summary of the historical patterns they suggest.

The graphs below provide some indication of the consistency of the various data sources as well as an historical perspective on mergers and acquisitions.

The FTC data are a basic source for research in merger activity. Figure 2.1 shows the annual FTC data for the number of large mining and manufacturing mergers and for "all" mining and manufacturing mergers (the broader series). As can be seen, the two series suggest similar patterns in merger activity. Both show an increase in the mid-1950s, a more gradual rise in the late 1950s and early 1960s, and then a sharp increase in the late 1960s (the "go-go" years),[10] followed by a steep decline in the early 1970s and another increase in the late 1970s.

It has been argued that it is the value of assets acquired by merger that matters, not just the number of firms. In fact, figure 2.2 indicates that both sets of data suggest similar patterns. Figure 2.2 shows annual data for both the number of mergers and the real value in 1982 dollars[11] of the assets acquired, as measured by the FTC "large firm" series. Movements in the two series are fairly closely correlated, and both series clearly show the peak of the "go-go" years.

As noted above, the major drawback of the FTC data for our purposes is their failure to include data on the current merger wave. In order to place recent experience in perspective, we need to "splice" the more recent data onto an appropriate FTC series. Figure 2.3 shows the annual number of mergers measured by the "broad" FTC series and by the annual series from the periodical *Mergers and Acquisitions* covering the purchases of domestic companies. These two series appear to track each other reasonably well, with both showing the peak in the late 1960s. The *M&A* series clearly indicates the boom of the 1980s.

Similarly, figure 2.4 presents quarterly data for the number of mergers measured by the FTC "large firm" series and by the *M&A* "domestic firm" series. These series, too, appear to track each other well.

Figure 2.5 allows us to compare the quarterly data from current sources. It presents the Grimm quarterly data on the number of mergers, along with the "domestic firm" quarterly series from *M&A* and the more comprehensive quarterly series

"Large Firm" Series

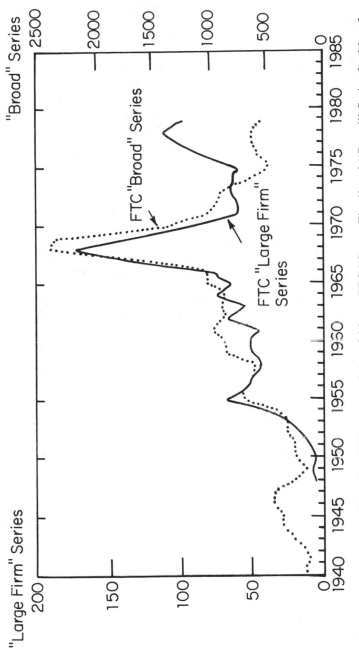

"Broad" Series

Fig. 2.1   Annual Number of Mergers and Acquisitions: FTC "Large Firm" and "Broad" Series for Manufacturing and Mining

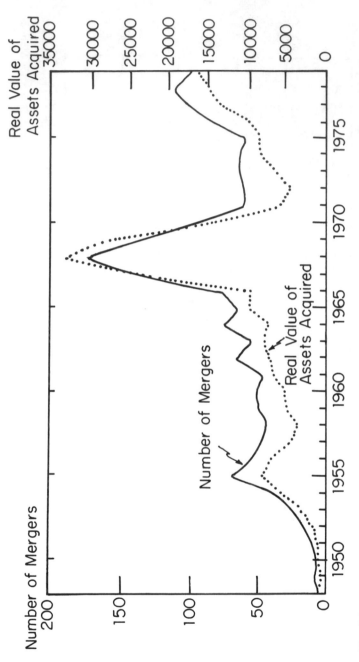

Fig. 2.2   Annual Number of Mergers and Acquisitions and Real Value of Assets Acquired (in millions of 1982 dollars): FTC "Large Firm" Series for Manufacturing and Mining

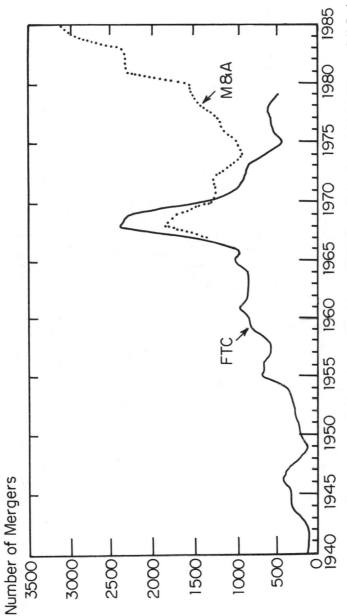

Fig. 2.3   Annual Number of Mergers and Acquisitions: FTC "Broad" Series and *M&A* "Domestic" Series

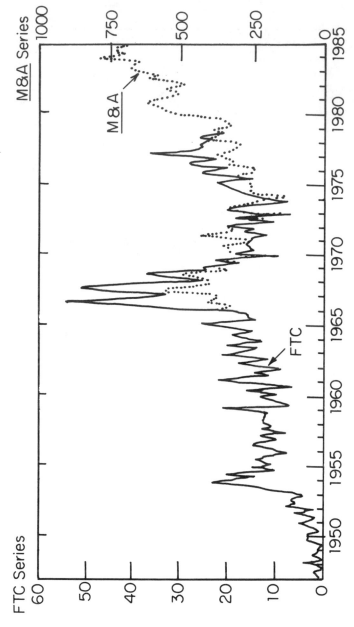

Fig. 2.4   Quarterly Number of Mergers and Acquisitions: FTC "Large Firm" Series and
M&A "Domestic" Series

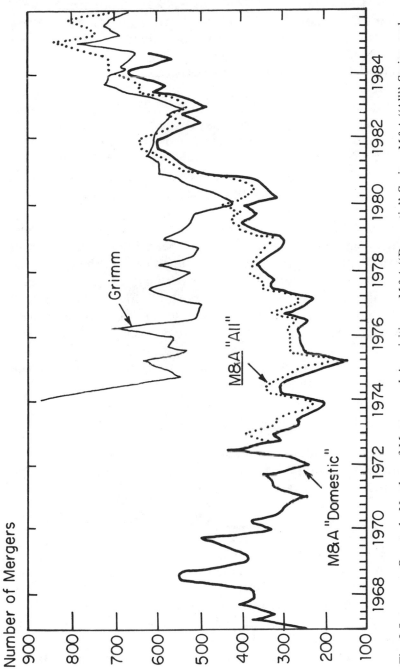

Fig. 2.5 Quarterly Number of Mergers and Acquisitions: *M&A* "Domestic" Series, *M&A* "All" Series, and Grimm Series

from *M&A*. The two *M&A* series track each other quite well, but the Grimm data diverge markedly from the other two series during the 1970s. The reasons for this divergence are unclear. As was explained above, the Grimm data have a lower cutoff point and pertain to announcements rather than completions. However, it seems unlikely that these differences could account for the divergence.

Finally, a longer perspective is provided in figure 2.6, in which the annual data on the number of mergers from Nelson, from Thorpe-FTC, and from *M&A* "domestic" mergers are all presented. The data show four noticeable peaks or "waves":[12] around the turn of the century, in the late 1920s, in the late 1960s, and in the 1980s.

Thus, the merger wave of the 1980s is not a wholly new phenomenon. Merger activity has been important in earlier periods. Indeed, when placed in the context of the lower real economic activity in these earlier periods, this earlier merger activity was relatively more important. Figure 2.7 provides this context, by dividing the data series shown in figure 2.6 by annual real GNP (in billions of 1982 dollars).[13] In essence, figure 2.7 shows the number of major mergers per billion dollars of real GNP. As can be seen in figure 2.7, the peaks of merger activity at the turn of the century and in the late 1920s were much more important relative to the size of the U.S. economy at the time than was true in the 1980s. Figure 2.8, in which the nominal value of assets acquired is divided by nominal GNP, tells a similar story: the merger wave at the turn of the century was much larger relative to the size of the economy than was the wave of the late 1960s.

2.3   Developing Hypotheses

We now turn our attention to the aggregate patterns of mergers and acquisitions described in the previous section. We ask whether there are fundamental economic forces that can explain a significant fraction of the variance in the quarterly or annual aggregate or merger and acquisition activity or whether, instead, this activity is driven largely (or entirely) by factors or elements that are not susceptible to economic analysis.

Our approach (since both authors are economists) is to start

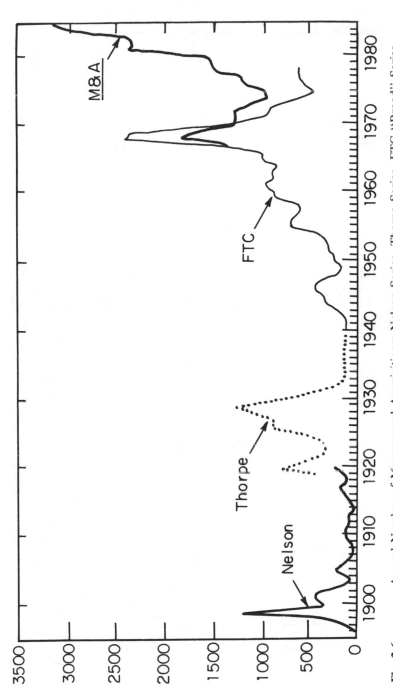

Fig. 2.6　Annual Number of Mergers and Acquisitions: Nelson Series, Thorpe Series, FTC "Broad" Series, and *M&A* "Domestic" Series

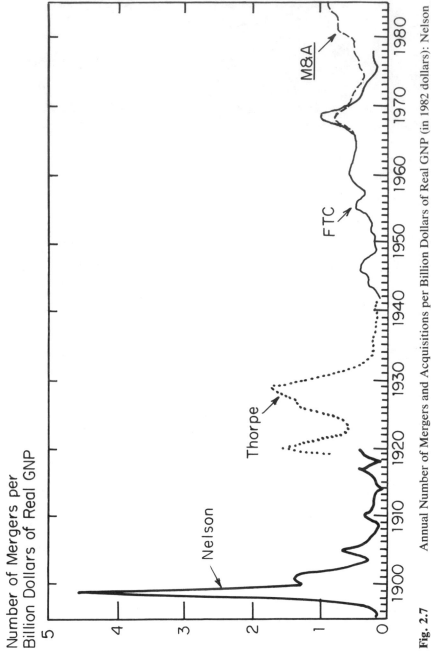

Fig. 2.7   Annual Number of Mergers and Acquisitions per Billion Dollars of Real GNP (in 1982 dollars): Nelson Series, Thorpe Series, FTC "Broad" Series, and *M&A* "Domestic" Series

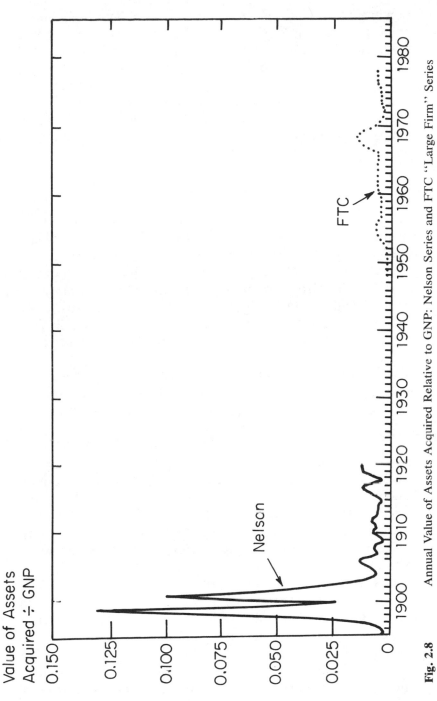

Fig. 2.8   Annual Value of Assets Acquired Relative to GNP: Nelson Series and FTC "Large Firm" Series

from basic economic principles and develop their implications for merger and acquisition activity. These implications become hypotheses that can be tested through statistical analysis of the relevant relationships among the data series. (A failure to find significant statistical relationships could indicate improper specifications of the hypotheses, poor data for testing, or true randomness in the phenomena being investigated.) In this section we develop the hypotheses; in the following section we report some preliminary efforts at empirical verification.

2.3.1   The Determinants of Merger and Acquisition Activity

A merger or acquisition usually constitutes an act of investment by the purchasing firm or individuals. But a merger or acquisition is an *exchange* of *existing* assets (a purchaser pays cash for the plant, equipment, personnel, and goodwill of an existing firm), whereas investment flows (at least, as defined by the GNP accounts) involve the creation of *new* plant and equipment. Consequently, we will focus primarily on the forces that cause individuals or firms to exchange assets among themselves.[14]

Asset exchanges should occur when purchasers believe that current prices for the assets constitute "bargains." One rough indicator of whether a company can be purchased at a "bargain" price would be a comparison of the purchase price with the likely replacement costs of the company's assets.[15] The lower the ratio of the former to the latter (other things being equal), the greater is the bargain, and the greater is the likelihood that some potential purchaser will prefer to buy the company and invest de novo. This ratio of purchase price to replacement cost, when expressed as the ratio of the current stock market value of a company (or of all companies in an industry, a sector, or the entire economy) to its replacement cost, is frequently known as "Tobin's q" or just "q."[16] Thus, the level of q for the economy during a given time period should be an important determinant of the aggregate level of merger and acquisition activity in the same period.[17]

Further, periods during which there are significant amounts of new information or unexpected changes in economic conditions, resulting in greater divergences of opinion among market participants as to the future prospects of a company, should be periods of greater aggregate mergers and acquisitions. In essence, when there are greater divergences of opinion, there is a greater likelihood that a prospective purchaser will be more optimistic about a company's future possibilities than will the company's current owner or owners and hence a greater likelihood that a merger or acquisition will occur.

In addition, the real cost of capital (capital costs that have been corrected for expected inflation) should be a determinant of aggregate merger and acquisition activity, since capital costs can influence the timing, financing costs, and expected profitability of these transactions. Tax policy should affect merger and acquisition activity, since various tax policies can affect the prospective profitability of various transactions, and affect it differentially for prospective purchasers and current owners. The overall size of the economy should also affect the level of merger and acquisition activity, since a larger economy will likely have more companies that could possibly merge with each other.

Finally, in the presence of inflation a fixed lower cutoff point for the inclusion of a merger or acquisition into a recorded data series (discussed in section 2.2 above) creates a false impression of an increase in mergers and acquisitions over time. It is necessary to correct for this upward bias over time for any empirical testing of hypotheses.

In summary, then, we expect aggregate merger and acquisitions activity to be related to: the ratio of market value to replacement costs (q); the level of divergence of opinion about future prospects; real interest rates (a proxy for capital costs); tax policy; the size of the economy; and a correction factor for the fixed cutoff point for the inclusion of mergers in data series.

2.3.2 Further Considerations of "q"

To the extent that the level of aggregate merger and acquisition activity affects the market value of securities (the numerator of q), there is an interactive or simultaneous relationship between q and the level of merger and acquisition activity; in other words, the level of q affects the level of these transactions, but they, in turn (and simultaneously), affect q.

In order to explain statistically the impact of q on mergers, we must simultaneously consider the determinants of q.

Since q is a measurement of the ratio of prices to costs at one point in time, whereas merger and acquisition activity is measured as a flow over a period of time (a quarter or a year), it is the *change* in q between two points in time that should be affected by the level of merger and acquisition activity during that time period. Further analysis of the components of changes in q between two points in time indicates that other influences—specifically, the level of real GNP, any unexpected changes in real GNP, the level of real interest rates, any unexpected changes in real interest rates, the capital stock at the end of the period, and the value of q at the beginning of the period—should also be important.[18]

Thus, for the purposes of empirical testing of the hypotheses advanced in this section, we need to employ statistical methods that allow for the simultaneous interaction between our two key variables and for the additional explanatory power of the other influences on these two variables.

2.4   Some Preliminary Empirical Findings

In this section we report the results of our preliminary efforts to test empirically the hypotheses developed in the previous section.

2.4.1   Efforts to Explain the Level of Merger and Acquisition Activity

We focused our attention on a single merger and acquisition data series: the quarterly FTC "large firm" series for 1948–79, which reports the numbers of mergers in the manufacturing and mining sectors in which the assets of the acquired company were at least $10 million and information concerning the merger was publicly available. This series offered us the maximum number of observations and the best overlap with other relevant data series.

As was discussed in section 2.3, periods in which there are greater divergences of opinion about companies' future prospects are also periods in which the level of merger and acquisition activity is likely to be greater. These same conditions should also cause the volume of trading on stock exchanges to be greater. Thus, we should expect to see a strong positive correlation between the level of merger and acquisition activity and the volume of trading. In fact, the simple correlation between FTC quarterly series and the quarterly volume of trading on the New York Stock Exchange for 1948–79 was $r = 0.52$.[19] Thus, merger and acquisition activity does appear to be driven by the same information and divergence-of-opinion influences that drive stock market trading volume.[20]

The discussion in section 2.3 indicated the other variables that should affect merger and acquisition activity: Tobin's q, real interest rates, tax policy, the general size of the economy, and a correction for the unchanged inclusion cutoff limit. (This last variable, of course, should only affect *reported* merger and acquisition activity.) Tobin's q and tax policy were combined into a tax-adjusted q;[21] as a proxy for capital costs, a real interest rate variable was constructed by subtracting the inflation rate (measured by the percentage change in the GNP deflator) from the interest rate on seasoned corporate Aaa bonds for the same quarter; and the size-of-economy and correction factor variables were proxied together by the level of nominal GNP.

We then applied regression analysis to determine how well these variables performed in explaining the quarterly pattern of mergers and acquisitions. Initially using ordinary least squares regression (which neglects the possible simultaneous relationship between mergers and q, discussed in section 2.3), we found the following results: the tax-adjusted q was positively and significantly related to mergers and acquisitions (contrary to our expectations) as was nominal GNP (consistent with our expectations). Real interest rates were negatively but not significantly related to mergers and acquisitions (consistent with our expectations). The overall explanatory power of the statistical relationship was quite good.[22] Similar results were obtained when two-stage least squares analysis was applied.[23]

2.4.2   Efforts to Explain "q"

As was discussed in section 2.3, changes in q from one point in time to another should be related to the following variables:

the level of merger and acquisition activity, real GNP, unexpected changes in real GNP, real interest rates, unexpected changes in real interest rates, the level of q at the first point in time, and the size of the real capital stock at the second point in time.[24]

We applied ordinary least squares analysis to determine how well these variables explained the quarterly pattern of changes in q. We found the following results: The level of merger and acquisition activity and the level of real GNP were both positively but not significantly related to changes in q (the former consistent with our expectations, the latter contrary to them). Unexpected changes in real GNP and real interest rates were both positively and significantly related to changes in q (which was consistent). Unexpected changes in real interest rates and the lagged value of q were both negatively and significantly related to changes in q (consistent). The concurrent level of the real capital stock was negatively (but not significantly) related (consistent). The overall explanatory power of the relationship was good.[25]

Overall, these preliminary results are encouraging. Merger and acquisition activity does not appear to be a random process. Rather, the data indicate that mergers and acquisitions respond to economic influences in some of the ways that we have suggested, although the positive relationship with Tobin's q remains a puzzle. Also, efforts to explain the pattern of changes in q (which are of interest because q itself has a simultaneous and interactive influence on mergers and acquisitions) yielded results that were mostly sensible.

2.5   Conclusions

The patterns of merger and acquisition activity are interesting phenomena for economic analysis. A better understanding of these phenomena should improve our knowledge of the operation of capital markets and of the economy in general. In this paper we have described these patterns, developed testable hypotheses, and reported preliminary empirical findings. We have also discussed the criticisms that have been directed at merger and acquisition activity.

We believe that merger and acquisition activity can be largely explained by the theoretical and empirical tools of economic analysis and that our findings point in a sensible direction. We expect that future work in this area should expand the base of knowledge and understanding about these processes.

Notes

We would like to thank Charles Larson for his research assistance.

1. For recent cross-section studies, see Harris et al. (1982), Wansley et al. (1983), Hasbrouck (1985), and Knoeber (1986).

2. The only recent work of which we are aware is that of Melicher et al. (1983) and Shugart and Tollison (1984). An older literature can be found in Markham (1955) and Nelson (1959).

3. The last report, covering 1979 and earlier years, is U.S. FTC (1981).

4. Curiously, the FTC published information on the value of acquired assets in mergers including those for which public information was not available, but it did not publish annual data on the numbers of these mergers.

5. The annual data can be found in U.S. Department of Commerce (1976) and various annual issues of the FTC's *Statistical Report on Mergers and Acquisitions*. The quarterly data can be found in Nelson (1959, 167–69).

6. See Nelson (1959).

7. Unfortunately, the annual and quarterly series are not consistent with each other. The annual series appears to be more complete.

8. Nelson describes these as "disappearances" and as "capitalizations," respectively.

9. See Nelson (1959, 166–67).

10. See Brooks (1973).

11. The GNP deflator, with 1982 = 1.0, was used to deflate the nominal dollar series.

12. Shugart and Tollison (1984) argue that the historical pattern of mergers and acquisitions is best described as a first order autoregressive process, with drift, and that their results are inconsistent with a characterization of the pattern as one of waves. Since they never formally define waves nor formally test a wave hypothesis, we are not convinced by their latter claim.

13. Ideally, we would like some measure of the potential number of mergers in any period. Absent a reliable measure of the number of business enterprises, we use GNP as a proxy.

14. A merger or acquisition of a firm usually entails one extra element—control over management—that other exchanges of assets (e.g., purchases of smaller blocks of shares in a company) do not have. For a discussion of the influences on the trading volume of shares of stock, see Epps (1975), Epps and Epps (1976), Verrecchia (1981), Tauchen and Pitts (1983), and Smirlock and Starks (1985).

15. To the extent that replacement costs only encompass physical assets, this type of measure will ignore intangible goodwill.

16. This ratio is frequently associated with the work of economics Nobel prize winner James Tobin. See Tobin (1969).

17. This approach is consistent with recent cross-sectional findings on the characteristics of takeover targets. See Hasbrouck (1985). Since q is the ratio of market value to replacement cost, "bargains" should appear

when market value is low relative to replacement costs, and hence merger and acquisition activity should be negatively related to q. By contrast, Melicher et al. (1983) predict a positive relationship between mergers and stock market prices. They believe that higher stock market prices are indicators of expectations of prosperity and that the latter are conducive to merger activity. Their justification for this latter link, however, is never fully stated.

18.   If we let i = 1,2 represent points in time and $q_i = V_i/K_i$, where V is market value and K is replacement costs, then it is easily shown that $\Delta q = q_2 - q_1 = (\Delta V - q_1 \cdot \Delta K)/K_2$. ΔK is current investment (I), and the influences mentioned in the text (other than q_1 and K_2) are the behavioral determinants of ΔV and I.

19.   The simple correlation between mergers and the natural logarithm of stock market volume was r = 0.66.

20.   It has been suggested that trading volume might be considered as a proxy for these information and divergence-of-opinion influences and thus be used as an explanatory variable for the level merger and acquisition activity. However, Verrecchia (1981) argues that, in general, we cannot infer lack of consensus from trading volume. Hence, we have not included trading volume in the analysis below.

21.   This variable can be found in Bernanke et al. (1985).

22.   Adjusted $\bar{R}^2$ was 0.74.

23.   The additional instruments for the second stage estimation of q were real GNP and the size of the real capital stock, plus the appropriate lagged variables.

24.   All variables are on a quarterly basis. The tax-adjusted q and real interest rate were constructed as before. The series for unexpected changes in real GNP and in real interest rates were constructed from first-order Box-Jenkins procedures. See Box and Jenkins (1976). The real capital stock came from the Citibase data file.

25.   Adjusted $\bar{R}^2$ was 0.15.

References

Bernanke, Ben, Henning Bohn, and Peter C. Reiss. 1985. "Alternative Non-nested Specification Tests of Time Series Investment Models." Unpublished manuscript, April.

Box, G. E. P., and G. M. Jenkins. 1976. *Time Series Analysis, Forecasting and Control*. San Francisco: Holden, Day.

Brooks, John. 1973. *The Go-Go Years*. New York: Waybright and Talley.

Epps, Thomas W. 1975. "Security Price Changes and Transaction Volumes: Theory and Evidence." *American Economic Review* 65 (September): 586–97.

Epps, Thomas W., and Mary L. Epps. 1976. "The Stochastic Dependence of Security Price Changes and Transactions Volumes: Implications for the Mixture-of-Distributions Hypothesis." *Econometrica* 44 (March): 305–21.

Harris, Robert S., John F. Steward, and Willard T. Carleton. 1982. "Financing Characteristics of Acquired Firms." In Michael Keenan and Lawrence J. White, eds., *Mergers and Acquisitions: Current Problems in Perspective*, pp. 223–41. Lexington, Mass.: Heath.

Hasbrouck, Joel. 1985. "The Characteristics of Takeover Targets." *Journal of Banking and Finance* 9 (September): 351–62.

Knoeber, Charles R. 1986. "Golden Parachutes, Shark Repellants, and Hostile Tender Offers." *American Economic Review* 76 (March): 155–67.

Markham, Jesse. 1955. "Survey of the Evidence and Findings on Mergers." In National Bureau of Economic Research, *Business Concentration and Price Policy*, pp. 141–82. Princeton, N.J.: Princeton University Press.

Melicher, Ronald W., Johannes Ledolter, and Louis J. D'Antonio. 1983. "A Time Series Analysis of Aggregate Merger Activity," *Review of Economics and Statistics* 65 (August): 423–30.

Nelson, Ralph L. 1959. *Merger Movements in American Industry, 1895–1956*, Princeton, N.J.: Princeton University Press.

Shugart, William F., II, and Robert D. Tollison. 1984. "The Random Character of Merger Activity." *Rand Journal of Economics* 15 (Winter): 500–509.

Smirlock, Michael, and Laura Starks. 1985. "A Further Examination of Stock Price Changes and Transaction Volume." *Journal of Financial Research* 8 (Fall): 217–25.

Tauchen, George E., and Mark Pitts. 1983. "The Price Variability-Volume Relationship on Speculative Markets." *Econometrica* 51 (March): 485–505.

Tobin, James. 1969. "A General Equilibrium Approach to Monetary Theory." *Journal of Money, Credit, and Banking* 1 (February): 15–29.

U.S. Department of Commerce. 1976. *Historical Statistics of the United States, Colonial Times to 1970*. Washington, D.C.

U.S. Federal Trade Commission. Bureau of Economics. 1981. *Statistical Report on Mergers and Acquisitions, 1979*. Washington, D.C. July.

Verrecchia, Robert E. 1981. "On the Relationship Between Volume Reaction and Consensus of Investors: Implications for Interpreting Tests of Information Content." *Journal of Accounting Research* 19 (Spring): 271–83.

Wansley, James W., Rodney L. Roenfeldt, and Phillip L. Cooley. 1983. "Abnormal Returns from Merger Profiles." *Journal of Financial and Quantitative Analysis* 18 (June): 149–62.

3 An Overview of Takeover Defenses

Richard S. Ruback

3.1 Introduction

Takeover defenses include all actions by managers to resist having their firms acquired. Attempts by target managers to defeat outstanding takeover proposals are overt forms of takeover defenses. Resistance also includes actions that occur before a takeover offer is made which make the firm more difficult to acquire.

The intensity of the defenses can range from mild to severe. Mild resistance forces bidders to restructure their offers, but does not prevent an acquisition or raise the takeover price substantially. Severe resistance can block takeover bids, thereby giving the incumbent managers of the target firm veto power over acquisition proposals.

A natural place to begin the analysis of takeover defenses is with the wealth effects of takeovers. There is broad agreement that being a takeover target substantially increases the wealth of shareholders. Historical estimates of the stock price increases of target firms are about 20 percent in mergers and about 30 percent in tender offers.[1] More recently, premiums have exceeded 50 percent. It does not require a lot of complicated analysis to determine that the right to sell a share of stock for 50 percent more than its previous market price benefits target shareholders.

At first glance, the large' gains for target stockholders in takeovers seems to imply that all takeover resistance is bad.

Richard S. Ruback is an associate professor of finance at the Sloan School of Management, Massachusetts Institute of Technology.

Resistance makes the firm more difficult to acquire. If the defense works, it lowers the probability of a takeover and stockholders are thus less likely to receive takeover premiums. Even for an economist, it is hard to argue that shareholders benefit by reducing their chance to sell shares at a premium.

But the issue is not that simple. Takeover resistance can benefit shareholders. Stockholders are concerned about the market value of the firm. The market value of any firm is the sum of two components: the value of the firm conditional on retaining the same management team; and the expected change in value of the firm from a corporate control change, which equals the probability of a takeover times the change in value from a takeover.

$$
\begin{array}{c}
\text{Market value} \\
\text{of the firm}
\end{array}
=
\begin{array}{c}
\text{Value of the} \\
\text{firm with current} \\
\text{managers}
\end{array}
+
\begin{array}{c}
\text{Probability} \\
\text{of a control} \\
\text{change}
\end{array}
\times
\begin{array}{c}
\text{Change in} \\
\text{value from a} \\
\text{control change}
\end{array}
$$

Stockholders are concerned about how takeover defenses affect all three components of value: the value of the firm under current managers, the probability of an acquisition, and the offer price if a takeover bid occurs.

While takeover defenses may lower the probability of being acquired, they may also increase the offer price. Furthermore, takeover defenses can affect the value of the firm even if it is not acquired, that is, the value with its incumbent management team. For example, consider a defense that allows incumbent managers to completely block all takeover bids. This would reduce the probability of a control change to zero and eliminate the expected takeover premium. The market price of the firm would then consist entirely of the value with its incumbent managers. This value arguably could be affected in two opposite ways by the takeover defense. First, the value could decrease as managers enjoy the leisure that the isolation from being fired provides. Second, the value could increase as managers stop wasting time and corporate resources worrying about a hostile takeover.

It is difficult to determine a priori whether takeover defenses are good or bad for stockholders. But one way to assess a takeover defense is to examine the rationale for resistance. Managers resist takeovers for three broad reasons: (1) they believe the firm has hidden values; (2) they believe resistance will increase the offer price; and (3) they want to retain their positions.

3.1.1   Managers Believe the Firm Has Hidden Values

The managers of most corporations have private information about the future prospects of the firm. This information usually includes plans, strategies, ideas, patents, and similar items that cannot be made public. Even if efficient, market prices cannot include the value of information that the market does not have. When assessing a takeover bid, managers compare the offer price to their own estimate of the value of the firm. Their estimate, of course, includes the value of the private information that they possess. When the inside information is favorable, the managers' per share assessment of value will exceed the market price of the firm's stock. Offer prices above the market price of the stock could be below the managers' assessment of its value. In such cases, managers would help stockholders by actively opposing the offer.

Opposition based on "hidden values" is in the shareholders' interests only when the private information is valuable. A problem is that the general optimism of managers about the future of their firms clouds their perception of values. Most top managers usually argue that their firms are undervalued by the market. They believe the market is systematically inefficient—it always underestimates the value of their firm. But this optimism, or distrust of market prices, is an insufficient basis for opposing takeover bids.

To qualify as a potential stockholder wealth-increasing reason to oppose takeovers, the inside information must be of the type that an investor would pay to obtain.

3.1.2   Managers Believe Resistance Will Increase the Offer Price

In most transactions in which there is disagreement about value, it pays to haggle about price. Corporate takeovers are no exception. In mergers, the managers of the target and bidding firms negotiate directly. In tender offers, however, the haggling generally occurs in the newspapers. The bidder circumvents the target's managers by making an offer directly to the shareholders. The target shareholders, therefore, lack a centralized bargaining agent. But takeover defenses can help: by making takeovers more difficult, resistance can slow down a bidder. This gives potential competing bidders the opportunity to enter the auction for the target firm. The most common form of this behavior is soliciting an offer from a "white knight" after a hostile takeover bid.

This auction seems to increase the final offer prices for target shares. Ruback (1983) reports that the final offer price exceeded the initial offer by 23 percent in forty-eight competitive tender offers during the period 1962–81. More recently, Bradley, Desai, and Kim (1986) find that stockholder gains are substantially greater when there are multiple bids. They report gains of 24 percent for targets in single bidder tender offers and gains of 41 percent for targets in multiple bidder contests.[2] Since takeover defenses can encourage competitive bidders to make an offer, these data provide some support for the view that resistance leads to higher offer prices.

Some managers use this rationale to adopt extreme antitakeover defenses that virtually prevent hostile tender offers. They argue that without the board as a centralized bargaining agent, shareholders will sell out at too low a price. Such a view presumes that the market for corporate control is uncompetitive and inefficient. The weight of scientific evidence and the casual observation of control contests suggests that such a view is incorrect. Furthermore, extreme forms of takeover defenses can have some relatively severe side effects because it prevents the removal of inefficient managers.

3.1.3   Managers Want to Retain Their Positions

If the bidding firm plans to replace the target's incumbent managers, the target's managers have little incentive to endorse the takeover proposal. Such an endorsement would guarantee that they would lose the power, prestige, and value of the organization-specific human capital associated with their positions.

In addition to the desire to retain their positions, managers are likely to have the natural belief that they are the best managers of the firm. Loyalty to employees also encourages resistance. Finally, being taken over can be considered a sign of failure: The premium indicates that the bidder believes it can manage the firm better than the incumbent managers.

In summary, takeover resistance motivated by the first rationale of hidden values and the second rationale of inducing an auction can benefit target shareholders, although the managers' natural bias is likely to result in opposition to some takeovers that would benefit target shareholders. The third reason for takeover defenses, managerial self-interest, benefits the stockholders only if resistance happens by chance to be the appropriate action for one of the first two reasons.

These three reasons for takeover defenses are not mutually exclusive—combinations of the three are often present in defense strategies. For example, managers may use takeover defenses because they prefer friendly, negotiated transactions. Negotiated acquisitions enable the target managers to share ideas and information with the bidding firm. Consistent with the first and second reasons, this may increase the offer price. It also increases the chances of retaining the target's management team, which is consistent with the third reason. Finally, a negotiated transaction is generally more civilized: to the managers that is like an increase in compensation.

There is very little general evidence to assess the overall impact of takeover resistance on stockholder values. However, Walkling and Long (1984) present some intriguing evidence: managers with large stockholdings in their firms are less likely to oppose takeovers than managers with small stockholdings. These data can be interpreted in two ways: either managers with large stockholdings oppose too little because they risk losing the big payoff from being acquired; or managers with small stockholdings oppose too much, because they care about their jobs and have no equity gains to offset the loss in compensation. While not resolving whether there is too much or too little opposition, the Walkling and Long study does suggest the importance of the effect of takeovers on managers in the decision process.[3]

The stock price evidence tends to focus on individual types of defensive actions. In the next section, I explain and evaluate pre-offer defenses. Section 3.3 does the same for post-offer defenses.

3.2 Pre-Offer Takeover Defenses

In this section I describe several types of takeover defenses that occur prior to an actual takeover bid. These defenses are summarized in table 3.1. The table contains a brief description of the defense and its defensive impact, whether shareholder

Table 3.1   Summary of Pre-Offer Takeover Defenses

Type of Defense	Description	Defensive Impact	Shareholder Approval	Stock Price Effect[a]	Potential Effectiveness
Staggered board	Board is classified into three equal groups. Only one group is elected each year.	Bidder cannot obtain control of the target immediately after obtaining a majority of shares.	Required	−1%[b]	Moderate
Super-majority	A high percentage of shares required to approve a merger, usually 80%. Board can void the clause.	Increases the number of shares required to obtain control in hostile takeovers.	Required	−5%*[b]	Mild
Fair price	Super-majority provisions waived if bidder pays all stockholders the same price.	Prevents two-tier takeover offers.	Required	−1%[b]	Mild
Poison pill	Rights to preferred stock issued to shareholders. Rights can be exercised after a tender offer or the accumulation of a large block of shares by an outside party. In flip-over plans exercised rights can be used to purchase stock in the bidder on favorable terms. In flip-in plans exercised rights are repurchased by the issuing firm at a substantial premium. The bidding firm or large shareholder is excluded from the repurchase.	Makes hostile tender offer prohibitively expensive.	Not required	?[c]	Severe

Dual class recapitalization	Distributes a new class of equity to stockholders with superior voting rights but inferior dividends or marketability. Allows shareholders to exchange the new shares for ordinary common stock. Allows incumbent managers to obtain a majority of votes without owning a majority of the common stock.	Required	2%*[d]	Severe

[a]An asterisk indicates statistical significance.
[b]See DeAngelo and Rice (1983), Linn and McConnell (1983), and Jarrell and Poulsen (1986).
[c]See Malatesta and Walkling (1985), Ho (1986), Kidder, Peabody (1986), and SEC (1986).
[d]See Partch (1986).

approval is required, the stock price effect, and its potential effectiveness. The stock price effects are my round number summary of the detailed empirical studies. An asterisk indicates statistical significance.

The potential effectiveness measure in table 3.1 is intended to capture the degree to which the defense would be effective, *assuming that the incumbent management team uses it fully*. I have described defenses as mild when they inconvenience bidders or force them to restructure their bids without raising the takeover price significantly. Severe defenses give the incumbent managers absolute veto power of corporate control changes.

The potential effectiveness rating will differ from the stock price effect in at least three circumstances. First, the market may believe that the courts will prevent the incumbent managers from using the device, so that a very effective device will be associated with a small stock price effect. Second, the stock price effect might be small for an effective device because the adoption was anticipated. Third, the stock price effect could be small because the change in the probability of being acquired, and thus the change in expected premium, is too small to be reliably measured for even a very effective device. This is most likely to occur when the firm is not the subject of takeover speculation.

3.2.1   Staggered Board Elections

In this corporate charter provision, the board of directors is classified into three groups. Each year only one of the groups, or one-third of the directors, is elected. This makes it difficult for a hostile bidder to gain immediate control of the target firm, even if the bidder owns a majority of the common stock. About one-half of Standard & Poors 500 firms have adopted this type of takeover defense.[4]

My estimate of the stock price effect of adopting a staggered board is -1 percent, which is not statistically significant. DeAngelo and Rice (1983) examine the stock returns for 100 firms that adopted antitakeover corporate charter amendments; 53 of these included staggered boards. They find no significant stock price response to the adoption of the amendments around the proxy mailing date. Similarly, Linn and

McConnell (1983) find no stock price effects for a sample of 388 antitakeover amendments around the proxy mailing date. However, they find significantly positive returns over the interval from the proxy mailing date to the stockholder meeting date. More recently, Jarrell and Poulsen (1986) report negative, but insignificant returns of about -1 percent for twenty-eight firms that have adopted classified boards since 1980.

Staggered boards are a moderately effective takeover defense. By preventing a majority holder from obtaining control of the board for two years, this defense hinders the bidder's ability to make significant changes in the corporation immediately. This limitation may in turn reduce the bidder's willingness to bid, and may increase the bidder's difficulty in getting financing.

3.2.2 Super-Majority Provisions

These corporate charter provisions require a very high percentage of shares to approve a merger, usually 80 percent. These provisions are also typically accompanied by lock-in provisions that require a super-majority to change the antitakeover provisions. Some super-majority provisions apply to all mergers. Others are only applied at the board's discretion to takeovers that they oppose or that involve a large stockholder. Hostile takeover bidders require a higher percentage of shares to obtain control of the target firm when the firm has a super-majority amendment.

The samples of antitakeover amendments examined by DeAngelo and Rice (1983) and Linn and McConnell (1983) both included super-majority provisions. Both studies found no significant negative stock price effects. But Jarrell and Poulsen (1986) argue that these earlier amendments did not generally include an escape clause for the board. They report that super-majority amendments with escape clauses are associated with a statistically significant return of -5 percent, whereas super-majority amendments without escape clauses are associated with insignificant returns of -1 percent.

In spite of the significant stock price response, I consider a super-majority amendment a mild takeover defense. Bidders can respond to this amendment by simply tendering for the whole firm. This need not increase the total cost of the acquisition. Without a super-majority amendment, a partial offer could be used to obtain control. In this case, all stockholders would tender and receive a weighted average of the offer price and the postexpiration price. The bidder can respond to the super-majority amendment by simply offering this average price to all shareholders.

3.2.3   Fair Price Amendments

In these corporate charter changes, a fair price is defined as the same price. That is, a super-majority provision is waived if the bidder pays all stockholders the same price. About 35 percent of firms have these amendments.

Fair price amendments are designed to prevent two-tier takeover offers. In such offers, the bidding firm makes a first-tier tender offer for a fraction of the target's common stock. The tender offer includes provisions for a second-tier merger. The merger price in the second tier is substantially below the first-tier tender offer price. This provides an incentive for stockholders to tender to receive the higher price. Since most stockholders tender, and since the bidder accepts shares on a pro rata basis, most shareholders get a weighted average of the first and second tier offer prices, or the blended price.

Jarrell and Poulsen (1986) report insignificant stock price changes of -0.65 percent for 143 fair price amendments. Consistent with this insignificant stock price effect, fair price amendments are a mild takeover defense. By requiring the same price for all shares, the bidder is forced to offer all shareholders the blended price. This restructures the offer, but does not raise the cost of acquiring the target.

3.2.4   Poison Pills

These are preferred stock rights plans adopted by the board of directors; shareholder approval is not generally required. However, the plans usually use "blank check preferred stock," securities authorized by stockholders and whose terms are determined by the board prior to issuance. In a poison pill, rights to preferred stock are issued to stockholders. The rights are inactive until they are triggered. A triggering event occurs when a tender offer is made for a large fraction of the firm, usually 30 percent, or after a single shareholder accumulates a large block of the firm, usually 20 percent. The triggered rights can be redeemed by the board of directors for a short time after the triggering event occurs. If the rights are not redeemed, they can be exercised. There are two different plans for using exercised rights: flip-over plans and flip-in plans.

In flip-over plans the exercised rights are used to purchase preferred stock, for, say, $100. The preferred stock is then convertible into $200 of equity in the bidding firm in the event of a merger. The primary effect of this plan is to raise the minimum offer price that shareholders would accept in a tender offer. For example, suppose a target's stock price was $50. Shareholders would choose not to tender their shares for any offer price less than the $150 payoff they would get from exercising the right ($50 of stock plus $200 of equity in the bidder minus the $100 cost of exercising the right). The minimum premium, therefore, is 200 percent.

In flip-in plans, the rights are repurchased from the shareholders by the issuing firm at a substantial premium, usually 100 percent. That is, the $100 of preferred stock would be repurchased for $200. The triggering firm that made the offer, or the triggering large shareholder, is excluded from the repurchase. This repurchase price sets a lower bound on the minimum offer price that shareholders will accept. It also dilutes the value of the bidding firm's equity position in the target. Flip-in plans often contain flip-over provisions that are effective for mergers.

Poison pills are relatively recent phenomena. Prior to the Delaware Chancery Court decision in 1985 that upheld the legality of the plans, there were only three such plans. Currently, there are over 200 poison pill plans. Because these plans are so new, there is limited empirical evidence on them. In a study of 12 early plans, Malatesta and Walkling (1985) find negative abnormal returns associated with the adoption of poison pills. Ho (1986) finds no abnormal returns for a sample of 23 poison pills. The SEC's study of 37 pills finds returns of -1 percent for all pills and larger negative returns for firms that were subject to takeover speculation. A study of 167 poison pills by Kidder, Peabody, and Company finds no stock price impact. But this study is methodologically flawed, so that its conclusions are unreliable. The impact of these plans, therefore, is currently unknown.

Both forms of poison pills are severe takeover defenses. These plans have the potential to insulate incumbent managers completely from hostile takeovers. The plans cannot be circumvented by restructuring bids. Flip-in plans are slightly more effective than flip-over plans because they prevent the creeping acquisitions of the type Sir James Goldsmith used in his attack on Crown-Zellerbach.

3.2.5 Dual Class Recapitalizations

These plans restructure the equity of the firm into two classes with different voting rights. Usually, the class with inferior voting rights has one vote per share and the class with superior voting rights has ten votes per share. The superior voting stock is typically distributed to shareholders. It can then be exchanged for ordinary common stock. The superior voting stock generally has lower dividends or reduced marketability; this induces stockholders to exchange their superior voting stock for inferior voting common stock. The managers of the firm do not participate in the exchange. This shifts the voting power of the corporation. Managers with relatively small equity holdings can control a majority of the votes after the recapitalization. This gives managers veto rights over control changes.

Firms with dual class equity are relatively rare. Partch (1986) reports that forty-three firms issued limited voting stock over the period of 1962–84. However, recently the New York Stock Exchange has requested permission from the SEC to change their one share, one vote rule to allow NYSE firms to adopt such dual class equity structures. These recapitalizations, therefore, could become much more common in the near future.

The empirical evidence presented by Partch (1986) is mixed. She reports a significant positive return of about 2 percent for the forty-three firms that adopted dual class plans. However, there are about as many increases as decreases in stock prices and the median is only about one-half of 1 percent. She concludes that the weight of the evidence suggests no significant stock price changes. Furthermore, these historical estimates may not be relevant for assessing the impact of a dual class recapitalization for a typical firm. As Partch emphasizes, the firms in her sample are atypical. They generally have substantial inside or family ownership; on average the managerial ownership was 49 percent of the firm prior to the recapitalization. Thus, the plans may not have substantially changed the probability of being taken over for these firms. The managers' approval would be required with or without the dual class equity.

Dual class recapitalizations can be very effective takeover devices. By concentrating voting power in the hands of incumbent managers, the device prevents bidders from obtaining control by tendering for the outside shares. Even if a bidder were successful in acquiring all of the outside equity, it would not have sufficient votes to replace the incumbent managers or merge with the target.

3.3   Post-Offer Takeover Defenses

After a bidder makes a hostile tender offer, the defensive actions include many of the pre-offer defenses, as well as several actions that can be directed at a specific bidder. Table 3.2 summarizes these post-offer defensive responses.

3.3.1   Targeted Repurchases

These transactions, popularly called greenmail, occur when a firm buys a block of its common stock held by a single shareholder or a group of shareholders. The repurchase is often at a premium, and the repurchase offer is not extended to other shareholders. Targeted repurchases can be used as a takeover defense by offering an inducement to a bidder to cease the offer and sell its shares back to the issuing firm at a profit.

However, evidence presented by Mikkelson and Ruback (1986) indicates that only about 5 percent of 111 repurchases occurred after the announcement of a takeover attempt. About one-third of the repurchases occurred after some less overt form of attempts to change control, such as preliminary plans for an acquisition attempt or proxy contests. Since two-thirds of targeted repurchases do not involve any indication of a brewing control contest, the classification of these transactions as takeover defenses is questionable.

Empirical studies by Dann and DeAngelo (1983), Bradley and Wakeman (1983), and Mikkelson and Ruback (1985a, 1986)

Table 3.2   **Post-Offer Takeover Defenses**

Type of Defense	Description	Defensive Impact	Stock Price Effect[a]
Targeted repurchase	Repurchase of block of shares held by a shareholder, usually at a premium.	Eliminates a potential bidder.	−3%[b]
Standstill agreement	Limits ownership by a given firm for a specified time period. May include an agreement with a large shareholder to vote holdings with the board.	Eliminates a potential bidder.	−4%[c]
Litigation	Suit filed against bidder for violating antitrust or securities laws.	Delays bidder.	0%[d]
Asset restructuring	Assets bought that a bidder does not want or that will create antitrust problems. Assets sold that the bidder wants.	Makes the target less valuable.	−2%*[c,e]
Liability restructuring	Shares issued to a friendly third party or number of shareholders increased. Shares repurchased at a premium from existing shareholders.	Makes it more difficult to obtain the number of shares required for a hostile bidder to achieve control.	−2%*[e]

[a]An asterisk indicates statistical significance.
[b]See Dann and DeAngelo (1983), Bradley and Wakeman (1983), and Mikkelson and Ruback (1985a, 1986).
[c]See Dann and DeAngelo (1983).
[d]See Jarrell (1985).
[e]See Dann and DeAngelo (1986).

report significant stock returns of about −3 percent at the announcement of the targeted repurchase. But Mikkelson and Ruback (1986) report that this loss is more than offset by stock price increases associated with the initial purchase of the block and other intervening events. The negative stock price reaction to the targeted repurchase announcement, therefore, seems to be caused by the reversal of takeover expectations formed at the initial investment. Overall, the total return associated with these transactions, including the initial investment, intervening events, and targeted repurchase is 7 percent, which is statistically significant. Consistent with this positive overall stock price effect, repurchasing firms seem to have a higher frequency of control changes subsequent to the targeted repurchase.

3.3.2 Standstill Agreements

These agreements limit the ownership by a given firm for a specified period of time. The agreement may involve allocating a number of seats on the board of directors to the large shareholder. Also, the shareholder may agree to vote with management. These agreements serve as a takeover defense by eliminating, at least temporarily, a potential bidder. The shareholder may, however, gain some control over corporate assets through seats on the board. Thus, a standstill agreement is more like a treaty than a defense.

Empirical results by Dann and DeAngelo (1983) show that the adoption of standstill agreements is associated with a significant fall in stock prices of about −4 percent. Furthermore, Mikkelson and Ruback (1986) find that the negative returns in response to targeted repurchases are much greater when they are accompanied by standstill agreements. These agreements, therefore, seem to reduce the wealth of target stockholders. But this stock price fall could simply reflect the market's disappointment that an expected takeover will not occur. Like the targeted repurchase finding, the negative returns may just represent the reversal of favorable expectations.

3.3.3 Litigation

Perhaps the most common form of post-offer defense is to file some sort of suit against the bidding firm. Jarrell (1985) reports such litigation occurs in about one-third of all tender offers made between 1962 and 1980. The suits charge the bidder firms with fraud, violation of antitrust or securities regulations, and so on.

The litigation seems to serve two purposes. First, it delays the bidder, thereby encouraging the entry of competing bidders. Consistent with this view, Jarrell reports that the frequency of competing bids is 62 percent for tender offers involving litigation and 11 percent for tender offers without litigation. Second, the litigation encourages the bidder to raise the offer price to induce the target to drop the suit and thereby avoid legal expenses. Jarrell reports that the stock price effect associated with filing the suit is about zero, on average, for seventy-one such litigations. This suggests that the defense is roughly a fair gamble.

3.3.4   Acquisitions and Divestitures

These changes in the firm's asset structure can be used to defend against a takeover bid. Such tactics include divesting an asset that the bidder wants, buying assets that the bidder does not want, or buying assets that will create antitrust or other regulatory problems. Each of these actions make the target less attractive to the bidding firm, and reduces the price the bidder is willing to pay for the target. Data provided by Dann and DeAngelo (1986) for twenty such transactions indicate that they reduce stock prices by about 2 percent, which is statistically significant.

3.3.5   Liability Restructuring

Issuing voting securities can increase the number of shares required by a hostile bidder. Typically, the firm places these voting securities in friendly hands that agree to support the incumbent managers. Repurchase can also be used to reduce the number of public shares, making it more difficult to buy enough shares to obtain control. Such repurchases are often financed by debt issues that may make the firm less attractive to potential bidders. These restructures seem to reduce stockholder wealth. Dann and DeAngelo (1986) report stock price declines of 2 percent on average for thirty-one such restructurings.

3.4   Conclusions

I wish I could conclude that takeover defenses are generally good or bad for stockholders. But the answer is not that simple. Furthermore, there isn't enough evidence of experience with takeover defenses for precise conclusions. I do, however, think that the analysis and evidence support three propositions.

First, defenses that give incumbent managers the power to veto hostile takeovers seem to be harmful. Of course, there are circumstances where such defenses can help stockholders, but I think those circumstances are relatively rare. Poison pills and dual class recapitalizations are cause for particular concern. There may be a way to circumvent the power that the incumbent managers have with these defenses, but no one has discovered it yet.

Second, defenses that destroy assets are probably bad. This category includes assets sold below their values or assets purchased above their values simply to thwart a takeover. Similarly, liability restructuring to the extent that it interferes with investment also destroys assets. Once again there are circumstances where such actions may help stockholders, but these cases are very rare.

Third, defenses which do not give managers veto power and do not destroy assets, such as antitakeover corporate charter changes, are probably not harmful. These defenses may cause bidders to restructure offers. They may even result in slightly higher offer prices. Their major cost is that the defenses will reduce the benefit from being an acquiring firm and thereby reduce takeover activity.[5] However, there is no evidence that the frequency of takeovers has been reduced by antitakeover corporate charter amendments.

In summary, some takeover defenses seem to be harmful. Perhaps not surprisingly, the most harmful tactics seem to be the most recent innovations, such as poison pills. This is disturbing because these defenses are not subject to shareholder vote and thus are especially difficult to control. Of course, they may just *seem* powerful because participants in the market have not yet had the opportunity to design tactics to circumvent the defenses.

Notes

I would like to thank Paul Healy, James Poterba, and Nancy Rose for comments on previous drafts. The support of the National Science Foundation Grant #SES 84020677 is gratefully acknowledged.
    1.   See Jensen and Ruback (1983) for a review of the evidence on takeovers.
    2.   The stock returns are measured over the interval beginning five days before the first offer and ending forty days after it.
    3.   See Mikkelson and Ruback (1985b) for a more detailed discussion of management compensation and takeovers. See also Lewellen et al. (1985).
    4.   Frequency estimates are based on data published by the Investor Responsibility Research Center, Inc., Washington, D.C.
    5.   See Easterbrook and Fischel (1981a, 1981b), Gilson (1982), Bebchuk (1982a, 1982b), and Ruback (1984).

References

Bebchuk, Lucian. 1982a. "The Case for Facilitating Competing Tender Offers: A Reply and Extension." *Stanford Law Review* 35:45.
———. 1982b. "The Case for Facilitating Competing Tender Offers," *Harvard Law Review* 95:1028–56.
Bradley, Michael, Anand Desai, and E. Han Kim. 1986. "Gains from Corporate Acquisitions and Their Division between Target and Acquiring Firms." Mimeo, July.
Bradley, Michael, and L. Macdonald Wakeman. 1983. "The Wealth Effects of Targeted Share Repurchases." *Journal of Financial Economics* 11 (April): 301–28.
Dann, Larry Y., and Harry DeAngelo. 1983. "Standstill Agreements, Privately Negotiated Stock Repurchases, and the Market for Corporate Control." *Journal of Financial Economics* 11 (April): 275–300.
———. 1986. "Corporate Financial Policy and Corporate Control: A Study of Defensive Adjustments in Asset and Ownership Structure." Working paper 86-11. Managerial Economics Research Center of the University of Rochester, August.
DeAngelo, Harry, and Edward M. Rice. 1983. "Antitakeover Charter Amendments and Stockholder Wealth." *Journal of Financial Economics* 11 (April): 329–59.
Easterbrook, Frank H., and Daniel R. Fischel. 1981a. "The Proper Role of a Target's Management in Responding to a Tender Offer," *Harvard Law Review* 94 (April): 1161–1204.
———. 1981b. "Takeover Bids, Defensive Tactics, and Shareholders' Welfare." *Business Lawyer* (July): 1733–50.
Gilson, Ronald J. 1982. "Seeking Competitive Bids Versus Pure Passivity in Tender Offer Defense." *Stanford Law Review* 35:51–67.
Ho, Michael J. 1986. "Share Rights Plans: Poison Pill, Placebo, or Suicide Tablet?" Masters thesis, Massachusetts Institute of Technology, Sloan School of Management.

Jarrell, Gregg A. 1985. "The Wealth Effects of Litigating by Targets: Do Interests Diverge in a Merge?" *Journal of Law and Economics* 28 (April): 151–77.

Jarrell, Gregg A., and Annette B. Poulsen. 1986. "Shark Repellents and Stock Prices: The Effects of Antitakeover Amendments Since 1980." Mimeo, August.

Jensen, Michael C., and Richard S. Ruback. 1983. "The Market for Corporate Control: The Scientific Evidence." *Journal of Financial Economics* 11 (April): 5–50.

Kidder, Peabody, and Company. 1986. "Impact of Adoption of Stockholder Rights Plans on Stock Price." June.

Lambert, Richard A., and David F. Larker. 1985. "Golden Parachutes, Executive Decision-Making, and Shareholder Wealth." *Journal of Accounting and Economics* 7: 179–203.

Lewellen, Wilbur, Claudio Loderer, and Ahron Rosenfeld. 1985. "Merger Decisions and Executive Stock Ownership in Acquiring Firms." *Journal of Accounting and Economics* 7 (April): 209–31.

Linn, Scott C., and John J. McConnell. 1983. "An Empirical Investigation of the Impact of Antitakeover Amendments on Common Stock Prices." *Journal of Financial Economics* 11 (April): 361–99.

Malatesta, Paul H., and Ralph A. Walkling. 1985. "The Impact of 'Poison Pill' Securities on Stockholder Wealth." Working paper, Universitiy of Washington, July.

Mikkelson, Wayne, and Richard S. Ruback. 1985a. "An Empirical Analysis of the Interfirm Equity Investment Process." *Journal of Financial Economics* 14 (December): 523–53.

———. 1985b. "Takeovers and Managerial Compensation: A Discussion." *Journal of Financial Economics* 14 (December): 523–53.

———. 1986. "Targeted Repurchases and Common Stock Returns." Working paper #1707-86, Massachusetts Institute of Technology, Sloan School of Management, June.

Partch, Megan. 1986. "The Creation of a Class of Limited Voting Common Stock and Shareholder Wealth." Working paper, University of Oregon, May.

Ruback, Richard S. 1983. "Assessing Competition in the Market for Corporate Acquisitions." *Journal of Financial Economics* 11 (April): 141–53.

———. 1984. "An Economic View of the Market for Corporate Control." *Delaware Journal of Corporate Law* 9 (May–August): 613–25.

Securities and Exchange Commission. Office of the Chief Economist. 1986. "The Economics of Poison Pills," March.

Walkling, R. A., and M. S. Long. 1984. "Agency Theory, Managerial Welfare, and Takeover Bid Resistance." *Rand Journal of Economics* 15 (Spring): 54–68.

4   The Impact of Taxation on Mergers and Acquisitions

Alan J. Auerbach and David Reishus

4.1   Introduction

Throughout the recent wave of mergers, there has been no shortage of explanations for the increase in activity in the market for corporate control. Some explanations emphasize the positive role that mergers and takeovers play in the allocation of resources in society. For example, corporate acquisitions may lead to the replacement of a poor management team; they may facilitate the contraction of an industry in which no firm would voluntarily adopt a reduction in size; they may generate synergies through the combination of complementary resources.

Yet clearly there are also explanations that have negative implications for social welfare. The most obvious, of course, is a reduction in the level of competition in a market. The tax motive has also been mentioned frequently. To the extent that corporations and their shareholders reap windfall gains via tax reductions, the Treasury may be unintentionally subsidizing takeover activity that must be paid for by others in the fiscal system. It is noteworthy, however, that combining firms may also facilitate more efficient behavior on their own part by reducing their taxes. For example, wiping out tax losses may

Alan J. Auerbach is a professor of economics at the University of Pennsylvania and a research associate of the National Bureau of Economic Research.

David Reishus is an economist with the U.S. Joint Committee on Taxation.

increase the firm's incentive to invest, particularly when new investment brings large, immediate depreciation deductions and investment tax credits that can only be used by the tax-paying firm.[1] Moreover, the tax reductions that occur may not be appropriately described as windfalls. For example, if firms incurring tax losses are regularly targeted for takeovers, then many firms might be encouraged to take risks that result in such losses.

Whether tax incentives that encourage merger activity are desirable or not, it is important to know what their impact is. The U.S. income tax at the individual and corporate level imposes an extremely complicated set of provisions for mergers and acquisitions; the tax system is certainly not neutral in this area. But do taxes really play a significant role in the merger decision? Congress appears to have concluded that they do, having adopted provisions in the Tax Reform Act of 1986 that would limit the tax benefits from firm combinations. Yet there has been surprisingly little research on this question. This paper summarizes our own work to date on the topic. While we cannot offer definite conclusions, our preliminary results suggest that:

1.   Many mergers and acquisitions provide an opportunity for corporations and their shareholders to receive some tax benefits.

2.   In a small minority of cases, these benefits are large in comparison to the value of the acquired company, suggesting that taxes provided motivation.

3.   Even in cases where there are significant tax benefits, there is no strong evidence that they were the driving factors in the takeovers.

Once again, we must stress the tentative nature of our conclusions. We have not found that tax factors do not matter. But there is still a lack of convincing evidence that they are an important determinant of merger activity in the aggregate.

In the remainder of this paper, we will briefly discuss the potential tax benefits from mergers and acquisitions. Then we will describe our research on the importance of these tax benefits to U.S. mergers and acquisitions during the period from 1968 to 1983.

4.2   Taxes and Merger Activity

There are several different ways that companies may reduce taxes through a merger or acquisition, and tax benefits can accrue at both the corporate and the shareholder levels. However, in some cases the tax benefits from a corporate combination are also available by other means, and such benefits should not be attributed to the merger process alone.

4.2.1   Shareholder Taxation

Shareholders of an acquired corporation can receive many forms of payment when they sell their shares as part of a merger or acquisition. Such receipts may be deemed taxable or nontaxable. If they are taxable, then the shareholders must pay capital gains taxes on their gain over basis. If they are not taxable, then shareholders need pay no taxes until they sell the shares in the acquiring company that they receive as payment. The latter treatment is clearly preferable to the former from the perspective of the acquired firm's shareholders. It may also represent a net gain to shareholders relative to the no-takeover situation; they may be less likely to sell their shares in the new company and incur capital gains taxes than they would have been had no acquisition occurred. For example, if a small company is bought out by a large, diversified one, major shareholders in the acquired firm would have less need to sell some of their holdings to obtain portfolio diversification.

In exchange for the benefits obtained through avoidance of capital gains taxes, there are costs. To avoid taxes at the individual level, the corporate combination must qualify as a reorganization; that places certain restrictions on the transaction. Among the most important are that the consideration paid to shareholders in the acquired company be voting stock, and that the acquired corporation's tax attributes be taken over by the acquiring company. This severely restricts the ability of the acquiring company to use cash in the acquisition process, or to obtain the tax advantages associated with stepping up asset bases of the acquired company's assets. We discuss the latter problem further on.

Indeed, the use of cash might be attractive to the acquiring firm for several reasons. First, there is a nontax advantage to cash because it is relatively easy to use in a hostile tender offer. However, cash might also be attractive for tax purposes.

An acquiring corporation with sufficient cash for a transaction will have the funds available for distribution to its shareholders instead if it does not use the cash for the acquisition. These funds can be distributed in two ways: dividends and share repurchases. Dividends result in taxes which would be higher for shareholders of the parent firm than the capital gains taxes paid by the acquired firm's shareholders in a taxable transaction. Thus, a taxable cash transaction would result in lower combined personal taxes on the two firms' shareholders than a nontaxable stock transaction combined with an increase in dividends.

But firms can also repurchase their shares, and if they do so, the tax advantage of using cash in the acquisition would disappear. For many years, economists have been puzzled by the unwillingness of most corporations to use the repurchase route to reduce the taxes paid by their shareholders. In recent years, repurchases have become quite substantial, but this was not true historically. Thus, the existence of a net shareholder tax advantage in a cash acquisition rests on the theory that corporations find it easier to purchase other firm's shares for cash than their own.

In summary, nontaxable stock transactions may produce a tax benefit by allowing shareholders in the acquired company to attain a more diversified portfolio without realizing their shares and paying capital gains taxes. But such transactions may limit the size of corporate level tax benefits. Taxable cash transactions offer a tax advantage to shareholders only to the extent that they facilitate the transmission of cash out of the acquiring corporation at capital gains rates.

4.2.2   Corporate Taxation

At the corporate level, the tax treatment of a merger or acquisition depends on whether the acquiring firm elects to treat the acquired firm as being absorbed into the parent with its tax attributes intact, or first being liquidated and then received in the form of its component assets. As indicated earlier, a tax-free reorganization must follow the first path, while a taxable transaction can be of either type. Once again, each form of transaction has potential tax benefits but it is important to determine what benefits might have been available even in the absence of a merger.

Acquiring a firm as a collection of assets allows a stepped-up basis for the assets, with assets that are depreciable or depletable then receiving higher allowances than would otherwise have been permitted. Prior to 1987 the liquidating target company (and therefore, its new parent) avoided capital gains taxes that would have been due on the simple sale of assets. This benefit occurred through the "General Utilities Doctrine," which allowed liquidating distributions of property to shareholders (in this case, corporate shareholders) to be made without the payment of capital gains taxes by the liquidating corporation (the acquired firm, in this case). For some assets, such as machinery and equipment, this was not a major benefit, since gains would still be subject to the recapture of ordinary income taxes previously deferred through the use of accelerated depreciation. For others, however, such as business structures and mineral property, the gain could be substantial.

When an acquiring firm takes over the tax attributes of the acquired company, it does not get the opportunity to step up asset bases. It does get the benefit of any unused tax credits or tax losses that the target firm has carried forward, plus any "built-in" tax losses that the target will incur in the future. Such built-in losses occur in a corporation whose assets have high basis and projected depreciation allowances but little productive value. The use of such tax benefits is limited by various sections of the Internal Revenue Code that require the acquisition to have economic substance and also require either the continuation of the target's operations (in the case of a taxable transaction) or restrictions on the extent to which losses can be used (based on the relative sizes of acquired and acquiring companies).

Even with these restrictions and despite the existence of other channels such as leasing, the parent firm may be better able to use these tax benefits than the target firm would have on its own. This is confirmed in Auerbach and Poterba (1986), who suggest that firms with unused tax benefits in a given year are quite likely to still be in that position several years later.

However the assets and tax attributes of the acquired company are treated, an additional tax benefit may be obtained if the acquiring company has unused tax losses and credits: it may set these against the otherwise taxable income of the company it acquires. Restrictions on this practice are weaker than those on using the tax benefits of the acquired company. For example, the rule limiting the use of tax benefits in reorganizations would have no effect except in the very unlikely event that the acquiring company were much smaller than the taxable company it acquired.

A final tax incentive at the corporate level that may lead to mergers and acquisitions is the deductibility of interest on corporate borrowing. Since the interest deduction is always available to corporations, there must be some reason why an acquisition enhances its attractiveness. We can think of at least two reasonable explanations. First, target management might be overly cautious about borrowing, either because of its own interests or because of its fear of adverse shareholder reaction. The untapped tax gain available through additional use of debt capacity could motivate an acquiring company. Second, by integrating different operations, merging corporations could reduce business risk and make it possible for the combined entity to borrow more than the two companies could prudently borrow separately.

In summary, there are clear tax benefits available at the corporate level in the form of stepped-up asset bases and the increased utilization of tax losses and tax credits. There may also be gains from increased borrowing capacity, though here the benefits are more problematic.

4.3 Empirical Findings

To evaluate the magnitude of the tax benefits from mergers and acquisitions, we compiled a sample of large mergers and acquisitions that occurred between 1968 and 1983. Our collection method and public data sources are described in our earlier study (Auerbach and Reishus 1986). Most of our observations fell between the mid-1970s and 1982. Much of what we say below must be tempered by the fact that we have not yet focused on the very recent wave of merger activity, for which data have only recently become available.

In our sample of 318 mergers and acquisitions, the average capitalized value of the acquiring company (before the acquisition) was just under $2 billion, with the acquired companies having an average capitalization of just over $200 million. There was relatively little difference in financial structure between the two groups, with the ratio of long-term debt to long-term debt plus equity (at market value) averaging 29.7 percent for acquiring firms and 27.4 percent for those acquired.

A majority of the firms in the sample are in manufacturing: 65 percent of the targets and 74 percent of the parents. Of the remaining companies, 23 firms in energy and mining explorations were acquired, 10 of them by companies in the same industry. Only 1 company in energy and mining acquired a company outside the industry. Likewise in the transportation industry, where there were 19 parents and 21 targets, 13 of the mergers involved 2 firms in the industry. The same general pattern was observed in the financial industry, where, of the 16 acquired companies and 16 acquiring companies, 10 were matched.

4.3.1 Tax Losses and Credits

Under present law, a company which incurs a tax loss in the current year has two options. If it had sufficient taxable income in the three previous tax years to offset the current loss, it may carry the loss back to the earlier years and obtain an immediate refund. If it does not have enough recent income to do this for all of its current loss, it must carry the rest of the loss forward. Likewise with tax credits, the firm may have to carry unused credits forward if accrued credits exceed a certain fraction of the firm's taxable income before credits. The disadvantage of carrying losses and credits forward is that they do not earn any interest and they may expire. In addition, firms with liquidity constraints lose the immediate cashflow that such benefits would deliver.

Table 4.1 presents a cross tabulation that is useful in considering the potential importance of tax losses and credits in motivating mergers. In the table, we classify both acquired

Table 4.1   **Mergers by Tax Status**

Parent Group	Target Group				Total
	1	2	3	4	
1	199	20	13	28	260
2	7	0	3	3	13
3	19	2	4	0	25
4	9	3	0	8	20
Total	234	25	20	39	318

Notes: Group 1 firms have positive tax payments.
Group 2 firms have negative tax payments but no carryforwards.
Group 3 firms have tax credits but not losses carried forward.
Group 4 firms have loss carryforwards.
Twelve firms have both positive tax payments and tax loss carryforwards, usually due to a subsidiary not consolidated for tax purposes (primarily life insurance subsidiaries). These firms have been classified on a case-by-case basis.

and acquiring companies into one of four categories according to their tax status in the last completed tax year before the merger or acquisition. These categories are:

1.   Taxable; the firms paid federal income taxes and did not have any losses or tax credits carried forward. Such firms can use other firms' tax benefits to shelter income.

2.   Not taxable, but also without any losses or credits carried forward. This happens when businesses can carry all their current losses and credits back to an earlier, taxable year. Such firms offer no obvious tax shelter benefits to other firms, but neither are they likely to want to obtain such benefits to shelter their own income.

3.   Tax credits, but not losses, carried forward. These firms are either currently taxable or are carrying all losses back, but they have tax credits they cannot use.

4.   Tax credits and losses carried forward. These firms are currently not taxable and must carry losses as well as crediits forward.

For tax losses and credits to be of potential importance as incentives for merger activity, three conditions must be satisfied. First, these benefits must be present in a significant number of cases. Second, firms must have combined according to a pattern in which those with benefits (groups 3 and 4) joined those who could make use of them (group 1). Finally, the benefits themselves must be of significant magnitude.

As table 4.1 shows, the first of these conditions is satisfied. Out of a total of 636 firms involved in the 318 mergers (some of which appear more than once in the list), 104 were in group 3 or group 4. The second condition is also satisfied: there were 69 combinations of a group 1 firm with a firm from group 3 or 4. At the same time, the fact that 12 of the mergers and acquisitions occurred between tax-constrained firms (4 between firms in group 3 and 8 between firms in group 4) indicates the importance of nontax factors in the merger decision. Most of these combinations of tax-constrained companies were horizontal, within a single industry, where one would expect the fortunes of firms to be closely tied together.

To consider the third condition, that these benefits be economically significant, we can refer to table 4.2. In the cases where there were tax benefits available, we estimated their size as their value to the taxable firm in terms of the present value of taxes saved through the use of the existing tax losses and credits carried forward. As a fraction of the market value of the acquired company, the average gain was 13.7 percent, or 9.0 percent when weighted by the size of the acquired company. The (weighted) average gain was larger in the minority of cases where the tax losses and credits came from the acquiring company than from the acquired company: 14.3 percent versus 5.5 percent of the value of the acquired com-

Table 4.2	Potential Gains from Tax Benefit Transfer (as a percentage of target firm's market value)		
Number of Mergers with Potential Gain from: (by size of gain)	Target	Parent	Total
No gain	277	293	252
Below 5%	20	8	28
5–10%	7	5	12
10–25%	11	6	17
Above 25%	3	6	9
		Average Gain (of those with positive gain)	
Unweighted	12.7	15.4	13.7
Weighted	5.5	14.3	9.0

pany. Although these were the average gains for the 20.7 percent of mergers in which some benefits were available, the gains exceed 10 percent of the market value of the target in 8.1 percent of all mergers, or 39 percent of those with some gains present.

Thus, we found that benefits from the increased use of tax losses and unused credits were present in about 20 percent of the mergers and acquisitions in our sample. In about 8 percent of the overall sample, the benefits were significant (at least 10 percent of the acquired company's market value). We must now ask the most difficult question: how many of these combinations occurred because of the available tax benefits? This is the subject of our continuing research, so we cannot offer clear answers yet. However, there are two pieces of evidence that shed light on the question.

First, the number of firms with tax losses involved in mergers and acquisitions in recent years has been large, but so has the incidence of tax losses among firms in general. In our sample, of 37 mergers and acquisitions that occurred in 1982 and 1983 (for which we use tax data at the end of 1981 and 1982, respectively), 8 involved either a parent or a target with tax losses (that is, in group 4). In a comparable sample of large firms not limited to those involved in mergers, Auerbach and Poterba (1986) found that 7.6 percent had tax losses carried forward at the end of 1981 and 12.0 percent had losses carried forward at the end of 1982. The pure chance of a loss being present among either parent or target is thus roughly equal to that actually observed in the sample.[2]

Second, there is little evidence that among merging firms, the form of the combination depended on whether there were tax losses and credits available. If tax motivations were important, one might expect to observe a greater number of nontaxable transactions among mergers with the potential for transferring tax benefits; these are cases in which the potential for stepping up asset bases, available only through taxable transactions, would be of little value. Yet our statistical analysis (described in the appendix) has failed to detect any significant connection between the type of transaction (taxable or nontaxable) and the presence and size of these tax benefits.

We must conclude, on the basis of our evidence, that while the utilization of tax credits and tax losses could play an important role in affecting merger activity, there is no strong evidence that it does.

4.3.2 Basis Step-Up

There are a small number of celebrated cases in recent years where the step-up of asset bases supposedly played an important role in the acquisition process. Our estimates of the potential tax benefits from this channel (described in more detail in our earlier paper) are based on calculations of the total basis step-up that could be achieved on assets of the acquired firm not subject to recapture. The results suggested that this was not likely to be as important a benefit to merging firms as the utilization of unused tax losses and credits. In only seven cases could we identify gains in excess of 5 percent of the market value of the acquired firm.

Our statistical analysis also failed to support the notion that firms with sizeable potential gains from stepping up asset bases would be more likely to choose a taxable transaction in order to take advantage of these gains. However, we have less confidence in these conclusions than those reached above because we doubt our ability to accurately measure the gains from stepping up asset bases. The detailed asset information required for such calculations is not normally available publicly.

The little public information that does exist supports the conclusion that basis step-up is not typically important in larger mergers. One source says that of the 100 largest acquisitions since 1982 only 17 have elected to use the basis step-up, and the value of assets involved represents a smaller 13 percent of the total (*Mergers and Acquisitions,* 1986).

4.3.3 Leverage

As we indicated above, the tax deductibility of interest deductions in itself is not an incentive to merge. It is an incentive to borrow. Yet, there may be changes associated with merging that make borrowing less costly to the firm in some respect. One may certainly ask whether firms that merge borrow more.

Given the publicity that this topic has received, we were surprised to find that they do not. In our sample, we measured the debt-capital ratios (measured at market value) of firms before and after merger, comparing the combined ratio for the separate companies two years before the merger or acquisition to that of the single entity two years after the transaction. We chose to distance the dates of measurement from the merger date to avoid characterizing a very temporary increase in debt around the merger date as a change in underlying financial structure.

We found that the ratio of long-term debt to long-term debt plus equity increased in our sample from an average (weighted by size of firm) of 25.4 percent to one of 26.7 percent. This is not a very important increase given that it occurred during a period of generally rising debt-equity ratios. Where the acquired company's market value was relatively large, between 25 and 50 percent of the size of the acquiring company, there was actually a decline in the debt-equity ratio. This is contrary to what one might expect for mergers with large capital requirements. It is important to stress that these mergers did involve increases in debt outstanding, but also in equity value. It has been well documented that, taken together, the market values of the two involved companies increase through merger (for example, Jensen and Ruback 1983). Our estimates merely suggest that borrowing did not outstrip growth in value. If the recent merger wave involved increases in leverage in the aggregate, then this represents a deviation from recent historical performance.

4.3.4   Individual Tax Factors

We indicated that a nontaxable transaction could lessen the capital gains tax burden for shareholders of acquired companies. It is difficult to know what this burden would be without a detailed list of shareholder tax rates and holding periods. As a rough measure of the potential benefit of avoiding a taxable transaction, we used the percentage increase in the acquired firm's market value in the two years preceding the merger or acquisition. We found statistically that this measure had no impact on the decision between taxable and nontaxable transactions.

The potential tax benefits from using cash in a merger hinge on the acquiring corporation's being in need of a way to get excess cash out of the corporation without subjecting it to dividend taxes. It is difficult to identify which firm, if any, had this motivation, but we can identify some that probably did not: those that had issued new equity in the two years immediately preceding the merger or acquisition. It is hard to imagine any reason why such a firm, having recently obtained an infusion of cash through the sale of shares, would then seek to reduce its internal cash position. Indeed, we found this to be one factor that did statistically influence the form of the transaction. Firms that had recently issued new equity were less likely to engage in a cash transaction; perhaps the method of payment in acquisitions does play a role in helping firms regulate their internal holdings of cash.[3]

4.4 Conclusions

Our results suggest that, for mergers and acquisitions in the 1970s and early 1980s between large public corporations in the United States, the potential transfer of unused tax credits and tax losses was the most significant potential tax-related factor. This was particularly so in cases where the benefits were used by an acquiring company to shelter the income of acquired taxable companies. The benefits from stepping up asset bases are less discernible. Likewise, purported gains from increasing leverage appear to be refuted by the stability of debt-equity ratios measured before and after mergers.

Even where potential tax benefits have been identified, we have not yet found any evidence that they have played an important role in the structure and frequency of mergers and acquisitions. However, further research on this matter is needed before more definite conclusions may be drawn.

Appendix

The value and type of tax benefits available to firms would be expected to affect not only the incentive to merge but also, once the decision to merge has been made, the legal form of the merger. The choice of stock or cash as the means of payment, and the decision of whether to have a taxable combination or a tax-free reorganization, should be influenced by various tax aspects.

These tax incentives were discussed more fully in the body of the paper, but can be summarized here by the following hypotheses.

1.   High premiums paid, or low shareholder bases in the acquired stock, should lead to the use of stock as a form of payment. This defers the capital gains tax that would otherwise be payable by those selling their shares in the acquired company.

2.   Low book value of depreciable or depletable assets relative to market value should encourage a taxable transaction to take advantage of basis step-up. Since nontaxable transactions require the use of stock, we would expect to see cash used more often when book values are high relative to market value.

3.   The presence of substantial tax loss and/or credit carryforwards on the targets' books would encourage the use of these credits and thus make nontaxable stock transactions more likely.

4.   The use of cash should be greater where acquiring firms have not needed to go to the market for new equity funds, and less where firms have an apparent desire to disburse cash from the corporate form.

In order to test these hypotheses, we performed a logit analysis where the choice of cash or stock as the means of payment was the dependent variable. For 241 of the 318 mergers in our sample we were unambiguously able to determine the means of payment. These included 128 stock (nontaxable), 106 cash (taxable), and 7 stock (taxable). The remaining transactions included mixtures of stock and cash. Since so few stock transactions were taxable, we focused on the choice between taxable cash and nontaxable stock transactions. Within this subsample, one would expect cash to occur more frequently with low locked-in capital gains of the acquired stock, high basis step-up potential, low tax loss and credit benefits from the target, and excess cash held by the parent. Our measure of the locked-in capital gains is crude and was statistically insignificant. The remaining hypotheses may be evaluated using table 4.3, which presents results typical of the regressions we performed.

We tried three different measures of the available tax gains from the basis step-up at the corporate level. The first, described in the appendix of Auerbach and Reishus (1986), is based on an estimate of the difference between market and book values of business structure. The second is based on the difference between market value and book value of the firm, and the third is based on the accumulated deferred taxes, which to some extent reflects the excess depreciation taken on assets. None of these were statistically significant or im-

Table 4.3   **Form of Payment in Merger: Logit Analysis**

Independent Variable		
Constant	0.573*	0.460*
	(0.210)	(0.229)
Tender offer	− 2.620*	− 2.690*
	(0.662)	(0.662)
Hostile tender offer	− 0.019	− 0.028
	(1.14)	(1.05)
Missing tender offer (post-1980)	− 1.180*	− 1.200*
	(0.348)	(0.345)
Stock new issue	0.777*	0.806*
	(0.324)	(0.329)
Stock repurchase	− 0.443	− 0.402
	(0.612)	(0.623)
Basis step-up	2.10	
	(30.30)	
Tax losses and credits	− 4.15	
	(9.19)	
Tax losses and credits × limit	7.80	
	(20.5)	
Basis step-up/Target assets		2.07
		(2.18)
Losses and credits × limit/ Target assets		− 3.86
		(4.09)
Losses and credits × limit/ Target assets		7.41
		(7.00)
Pseudo-R^2	0.088	0.095

Notes: Standard errors are in parentheses.
* = significant at .05 level.
Dependent variable = 1 for stock transactions.

portant in explaining the form of payment. Only the results from the first version of this variable are shown in table 4.3. Likewise, the results for the tax saving due to use of losses and credits are not significant in explaining the form of payment. This is true whether we use the straight gains from the tax variables, or a version which attempts to account for the legal limitations that are due to the relative sizes of target and parent in a reorganization. In general, the standard errors of the estimated coefficients render them insignificant, often with a sign opposite from that predicted.

The variables which are significant in explaining the changes are the stock issuing or purchasing behavior of the acquiring firm in the period two years before the merger. A firm which has previously issued new stock in this period is more likely to use stock in the merger, and one that has retired stock is more likely to use cash. Also, if a tender offer was used in the combination, cash is far more likely to be used as the means of payment. This is true even when we control for the hostility of the transaction using dummy variables for management resistance and the presence of multiple bidders.[4] We do not have data on tender offers past 1980, and the dummy variable representing this period has a significant effect on the probability of cash being used, reflecting the increased use of cash in our sample after 1980.

In summary, there is little evidence from the logit regressions that the corporate tax effects we have identified are important in determining the form of the merger transaction. This does not imply that they are unimportant for the decision to merge. While the current results provide no strong support for taxes as an important motivation to merge, this can only be tested directly when merged firms are compared with firms that did not merge.

Notes

We are grateful to the National Bureau of Economic Research, the National Science Foundation, and the Institute for Law and Economics at the University of Pennsylvania for financial support.

1.   Auerbach (1983) and Auerbach and Poterba (1987) find that taxpaying firms face a greater incentive to invest in machinery and equipment than firms not paying taxes because of net operating loss deductions.

2.   Taking the two-year average loss frequency of about 10 percent as applying to all firms in the sample, one would expect 19 percent of the mergers to have at least one firm with a loss (10 percent targets plus 10 percent parents minus 1 percent to correct for double counting when both have losses). The observed incidence of 8 out of 37 is only slightly above this percentage.

3.   We are also aware, however, that baser theories of management behavior, such as "if you've got it, spend it, if you haven't, issue stock" are also consistent with this finding. In general, it is difficult to distinguish the argument that internal funds are a cheaper source of capital for tax reasons from the argument that they are cheaper because managers need not subject themselves to the judgment of the market.

4.   The data on tender offers was kindly supplied to us by Michael Jensen.

References

Auerbach, Alan J. 1983. "Corporate Taxation in the U.S." *Brookings Papers on Economic Activity.*

Auerbach, Alan J., and James M. Poterba. 1987. "Tax Loss Carryforwards and Corporate Tax Incentives." In M. Feldstein, ed., *The Effect of Taxation on Capital Accumulation,* pp. 305–38. Chicago: University of Chicago Press.

Auerbach, Alan J., and David Reishus. 1986. "Taxes and the Merger Decision." NBER working paper #1855, March.

Jensen, Michael C., and Richard S. Ruback. 1983. "The Market for Corporate Control," *Journal of Financial Economics* 11:5–50.

Mergers and Acquisitions. 1986. "The Threat of a Merger Tax." Vol. 21, no. 1, p. 19.

5 Management Buyouts as a Response to Market Pressure

Andrei Shleifer and Robert W. Vishny

5.1 Introduction

The early 1980s have witnessed a dramatic increase in management buyouts of public companies. In these transactions a team of investors including the managers borrow the money and buy the shares of the firm's public shareholders. Equity in the private company emerging from this transaction is owned by managers, investment bankers, institutional investors such as insurance companies, and sometimes Employee Stock Ownership Plans (ESOPs). But equity constitutes only a small fraction of capitalization: debt-equity ratios typically range from 6:1 to 12:1 (hence the term leveraged buyout). A management buyout (MBO) is a particular type of leveraged buyout in which management participates in a buyout of shareholders of a public corporation, as opposed to a private company or a division of a public or private company.

When an MBO takes place, shareholders earn a 50 percent premium on average and managers often take money out and still end up with larger equity stakes (in dollar terms) than they previously held. The sponsoring investment bankers pocket high fees and commonly realize 50 percent annual returns over five to seven years on their equity investment in

Andrei Shleifer is an assistant professor of finance at the Graduate School of Business, University of Chicago, and a faculty research fellow of the National Bureau of Economic Research.

Robert W. Vishny is an assistant professor of economics at the Graduate School of Business, University of Chicago, and a faculty research fellow of the National Bureau of Economic Research.

the new firm. With everyone doing so well, it is not surprising that management buyouts have grown.

And grow they have. While the first $100 million transaction did not occur until 1979, transactions in the hundreds of millions of dollars became common shortly after that, culminating in the $5.4 billion buyout of Beatrice Foods in 1985. The total dollar volume of transactions has increased from $1 billion in 1980 to $10 billion in the first six months of 1984 and is certain to be higher now. It is clear that the management buyout today is a relevant option for all but the very largest American corporations.

The amount of money changing hands in MBOs—whether going to shareholders, to managers, or to investment bankers—has promoted both curiosity and concern. Why are MBOs happening now, and in such large volume? What are the sources of gains that account for 50 percent or, in the case of MBOs in which several bidders are involved, 70 percent premia? Is it true value creation, or just value transferred from the old shareholders and the taxman? If it is value transfer, is the government footing the bill or are the selling shareholders getting ripped off? If, in contrast, value is created through cost-cutting and more responsible capital budgeting, why do we need MBOs to get this accomplished?

In this paper we attempt to describe and interpret what has been happening recently in a way that addresses these common questions and concerns. While data on private firms are hard to come by, and the skimpy data that exist have not been completely analyzed, some insights are beginning to emerge from case studies. In a nutshell, our interpretation of the evidence runs as follows. Inflation, tax law changes, and innovations in the market for risky, unsecured debt in the early 1980s have created new opportunities to increase value. Market values of many large corporations could be raised through recapitalizations, takeovers, and by other means. While some firms responded to the changing environment by voluntarily changing their operating strategies and financial structures, other firms faced a hostile takeover. In response to these threats, some management teams, committed to the perpetuation of their own control, undertook management buyouts. We therefore view many of these transactions as a response to the market pressure to restructure and recapitalize. While management buyouts accommodate the financial pressures of the market, they also allow incumbent management to continue running the business. Interestingly, the viability of the MBO as a takeover defense has been bolstered by the same capital market developments and tax advantages that have increased the pressure coming from hostile takeovers. We believe that these facts are responsible for many of the MBOs of the 1980s.

In the rest of the paper we develop this argument in greater detail. In section 5.2, we review the changes of the late 1970s and early 1980s and try to document the experience in the market for corporate control that we believe is a response to an excessively slow adjustment to changes in the environment. We show how that environment put pressures on firms and in many cases led to challenges to the control of incumbent management. Management buyouts have enabled management to defeat many of these challenges while still dealing directly with the problems that sparked the challenge. We also attempt to summarize the evidence on the question of the source of MBO gains, since tax savings, deviation of market prices from fundamental values, and efficiency gains all seem plausible. In section 5.3, we recapitulate our view of the MBO as a defensive response to market pressures and we discuss its consequences for economic efficiency.

5.2 An Explanation of Management Buyouts

5.2.1 Changes in the Economic Environment

The structural changes in the American economy in the late 1970s and early 1980s have increased the ease and profitability of acquiring old corporate assets. This has precipitated many forms of corporate control transactions, among them management buyouts.

One of the most important shocks hitting the economy in that period was inflation. As amply documented by Feldstein (1983), it had significant effects on the value and the deployment of corporate assets. First, inflation raised the nominal value of corporate assets above their historical cost. This created the opportunity to buy used assets and to depreciate them from scratch with a large step-up in basis. Such "churning" transactions became all the more attractive with the Economic Recovery Tax Act (ERTA) of 1981, which allowed for accelerated depreciation of newly purchased old assets as well as completely new assets (see Gordon, Hines, and Summers 1986). With only a small depreciation recapture and a large step-up in basis, churning used assets became an attractive option.

These transactions are especially advantageous from the tax viewpoint if the company selling assets is liquidated. Under the General Utilities doctrine (repealed in the 1986 tax reform), asset sales accompanied by liquidation are free from capital gains taxes at the corporate level. Thus, if a seller of assets survives as a corporate entity, it must pay taxes on capital gains realized from this sale, whereas if this seller liquidates in the process, such taxes are avoided. Not surprisingly, this provision has encouraged the churning of whole companies.

A second important consequence of inflation was the substantial reduction in real corporate debt obligations. Since interest payments were not indexed, a few years of rapid inflation substantially reduced the outstanding debt. This had two important effects. First, firms were ripe to lever up and take advantage of tax shields associated with the deductibility of interest payments. These interest tax shields may have also increased in value with the inflation-driven decline in depreciation tax shields. After several years of inflation, firms were clearly operating below their debt capacities. Second, the free cash flows of many corporations that were not too adversely affected by the reduction in depreciation tax shields may have increased as their revenues kept up with inflation while interest payments did not. As pointed out by Jensen (1986), the existence of large free cash flows can lead to corporate waste and self-interested capital budgeting decisions by management. While debt has the effect of encouraging managers to run a tight ship to meet their interest payments, the absence of debt gives them the freedom to waste money. By reducing real corporate debt obligations, inflation may have created both the opportunity and the need to lever up.

In addition to inflation, two other changes bolstered the market for corporate control. The first was improved borrowing opportunities, especially through the use of unsecured debt. Access to increasingly large pools of institutional funds through bank loans, junk bonds, and other arrangements made borrowing possible in many cases where it would not have been five years earlier. It is quite likely, of course, that the development of these markets was in part a response to the needs of corporate control transactions.

Another tax strategy that encouraged MBOs was the use of Employee Stock Ownership Plans. The 1981 ERTA raised the capacity of the ESOPs to borrow money from a bank, buy the firm's shares and then deduct both interest and *principal* payments on the loan. Effectively, this enabled the firm itself to deduct the principal on its debt, as long as that debt was channeled through the ESOP. To make ESOPs even more attractive, Congress passed a bill in 1984 allowing banks to deduct half of their interest income from loans to an ESOP. Some of this saving is undoubtedly passed on to the firm.

Inflation, better capital markets, and tax laws of this period created substantial opportunities for corporate raiders or incumbent managers to raise shareholder wealth through restructuring and recapitalization. Value gains could be realized by closing plants, curtailing diversification strategies, levering up, churning assets (especially whole companies), and bringing in ESOPs. Changes in the environment not only increased the pressure from hostile takeovers, but also made the management buyout a more viable defensive option, since better borrowing opportunities and large tax gains subsidized these transactions.

5.2.2 Management Response

Many companies voluntarily adopted value-increasing changes. Depressed stock prices and tax gains were probably sufficient to motivate these firms. But levering up and eliminating slack is not a proposition that is costless to management. Life becomes more difficult as management faces the constant pressure of meeting debt payments, the high cost of financial distress, and the loss of control over free cash flows. Furthermore, a management initiating an MBO puts the firm into play and may raise the probability of its being acquired in a hostile takeover. As a result, many management teams have chosen not to increase leverage to value-maximizing levels.

When hostile takeovers threatened the continuity of their control, target managements responded with the MBO (among other defenses, such as greenmail, scorched earth, and poison pills). Although executed under pressure, this transaction nonetheless accomplishes two goals. On the one hand, the enterprise survives as an independent entity under current management. On the other hand, tax and other benefits are realized, thus relieving the pressure for change.

5.2.3 MBOs as a Response to a Hostile Threat

The cases we have looked at largely support the proposition that MBOs are often a response to a hostile threat. We focused on the set of companies that were part of the Fortune 500 in 1980 and were acquired sometime between 1981 and 1984. We found that, of the eleven successful MBOs, six were responses to direct hostile threats, expressed either as actual tender offers or as acquisitions of shares with an intent to influence corporate decisions. In the subsample of seven failed MBO attempts, three were (unsuccessful) responses to the threat of a hostile takeover. At least for very large firms, the primary impetus behind the MBO is often not the prospect of making a large acquisition profit, but rather the threat that someone will do so at management's expense.

Perhaps it is evidence of the sweat and pressure following a successful MBO and of the risks of being outbid by a hostile raider that a significant number of MBOs are initiated only after a hostile threat. The drawbacks to such a takeover must be significant from management's point of view, for virtually every analysis of MBOs has found that value gains from these transactions are fairly large. DeAngelo, DeAngelo, and Rice (1984) find an average premium of 56 percent over the day earlier share price. Lowenstein (1985) in his sample of twenty-eight MBOs with purchase prices over $100 million also finds a 56 percent premium. In our sample of eleven successful management buyouts of Fortune 500 firms, we find an average premium over the day earlier market price of 53 percent. These results are consistent across samples, and are also similar to the findings for interfirm cash tender offers.

5.2.4   Sources of MBO Gains

Given the large premia being paid by investment bankers and institutional investors in MBOs, there seems to be a strong presumption that there are either large value gains from the new financial and ownership structure or large gains based on hidden values in the pre-MBO company. The three sources of gains that we think can plausibly account for a significant portion of the premium are: tax savings, improvements in efficiency (which would include value-increasing liquidation), and pre-MBO underpricing of the firm's equity relative to the old regime's expected future cash flows. Because the relative significance of these three sources of gains has been widely debated, we will examine their importance in some detail below, and give a few examples. First, however, we need to stress two important points that put these discussions of MBO gains in perspective.

The existence of potential gains from acquiring and/or restructuring the firm is what attracts a hostile bidder in the first place. It is therefore not surprising that these gains might be large; otherwise the hostilities might never have started. But the exact source of gains that has precipitated the hostile takeover is not necessarily the same as the source of gains from the defensive MBO. For example, a hostile takeover launched in order to force management to shut down unprofitable capacity may be defeated by a higher offer from MBO organizers who plan to get a larger portion of their value gains from tax benefits of leverage. Conversely, even when the initial impetus behind the MBO is a hostile tender offer designed to realize gains from market underpricing or tax savings, we would expect management to strive harder to cut costs and increase efficiency in the highly levered and more closely held new firm. Having paid a large premium, MBO organizers must find ways to realize value when constrained to meet large debt payments. Competitive bidding in the market for corporate control, and debt-equity ratios that range from 6:1 to 12:1, mean that this constraint is likely to be binding.

The other point is that the exact nature of the gains in an MBO bears little relation to whether or not the public shareholders have been coerced to sell. Whatever the source of gains, some coercion is quite likely to have taken place, in the sense that the public shareholders could not completely share in the expected gains *realized after the MBO*. The issue of coercion is thus different from that of MBO organizers buying underpriced shares. The latter applies when shares are acquired at a price below their fundamental value *under the old regime*. Coercion takes place when public shareholders would rather keep their current share of the post-MBO firm than take the price being offered. One way, but not the only way, for this to happen is if shareholders are forced out at a price which exceeds the prevailing market price but still falls short of the value of expected future dividends under the pre-MBO operating strategy.

The extent of coercion—whatever the source of gains—is hard to gauge. In the substantial fraction of cases with competing bids, there is reason to believe that, as in any auction, much of the gain accrues to those selling. In these cases, there is little coercion. Even when a bidder other than management does not surface, management's bid may have been set sufficiently high so as to deter the entry of competing bidders. Again, this would give most of the gains to public shareholders.

It is important to realize, however, that for an MBO to be profitable for its organizers, there must be some coercion— meaning that public shareholders do not capture all of the gains. Otherwise, what's in the deal for the organizers? While there is little real evidence on exactly how gains are shared between the organizers and public shareholders, there is some anecdotal evidence that managers do not volunteer to give up all of the gains.

For example, when Mr. Stokely attempted to take Stokely– Van Camp private, he offered $50 for shares that were selling for $38 prior to his bid. Eventually, however, the company was sold to Quaker Oats for $77, suggesting that perhaps Mr. Stokely had not offered all of the gains to his shareholders. In the same spirit, the management of Norton Simon originally offered $725 million for the company which fell far short of Esmark's $1 billion winning bid. In line with these stories, Lowenstein (1985) reports that average premia are 70 percent for successful MBOs in which three or more bidders are involved as compared to 50 percent for cases with fewer than three bidders.

In addition there is strong evidence for the incumbent advantage view, meaning that insiders have superior access to information as well as other strategic advantages in a takeover battle. Easy access to information is especially important in obtaining financing and ensuring profitable operation of the firm from the very beginning (which is a virtual necessity when the firm is highly leveraged). Other strategic advantages of the insiders include the ability to unilaterally lock up key assets (the crown jewels) with a friendly third party and having a much better chance of setting up an ESOP.

While the incumbent's advantage over other bidders somewhat limits the extent of protection afforded old shareholders by the competitive bidding process, aspects of that advantage also make for superior value gains from a properly structured MBO as opposed to a hostile third-party takeover.

Tax Gains

Having said all this, we return to a discussion of the sources of value gains. The most commonly discussed source of gains in MBOs is value transferred from the taxman (Lowenstein 1985), through deductibility of interest, step-up in asset basis for depreciation purposes, and the ESOP. To illustrate the magnitude of these potential tax savings, we consider four well-publicized examples.

Shareholders of Congoleum, Inc., were bought out in 1980 for $448 million, at a 50 percent premium over market. The estimated step-up in basis was $350 million against $26 million in recapture. Needless to say, tax savings were large.

Norris Industries went through an MBO in 1981 for $420 million, at a 48 percent premium. In the first year after the MBO, depreciation deductions increased to $33 million from $18 million a year earlier. Interest deductions increased to $62 million from $1 million the year before.

When management took Signode private in 1982 for $430 million (29 percent above market value one day earlier), they wrote up assets from $150 million to $300 million, thus raising total annual write-offs from $20 million to $60 million.

Dan River used its ESOP to buy 70 percent of the new company's equity. According to Lowenstein (1985), $100 million out of the total purchase price of $150 million could be ascribed to various tax savings, the premature liquidation of pension plans, and other sources unrelated to the company's operations.

Underpricing of the Firm's Equity

While the evidence for the importance of tax gains is fairly abundant, the case for the importance of underpricing of the firm's equity relative to fundamental value is much more tenuous. First, it runs counter to the efficient markets hypothesis, which has been the bedrock of financial economics for many years. Recent critics of that hypothesis include Black (1986), who now calls the market "efficient" as long as the price is within a factor of two of fundamental value. If financial markets are highly efficient, the notions of the bear market of the late 1970s and of cheap stocks in basic industries are not very persuasive. Even if they are not efficient, the gains from MBOs are still bounded by the size of the informational inefficiency in the market.

Weaker forms of the efficient markets hypothesis are consistent with managers having special information about their companies that enables them to know when their firms are underpriced even when the stock price is fully rational based on the market's limited information. Although such informational asymmetries would give managers an opportunity to buy undervalued companies *if* they could buy secretly, it is important to recognize that management's bid itself conveys a lot of information. Moreover, information is revealed when the MBO organizers try to obtain junk bond financing. In a competitive corporate control market, such information revelation severely handicaps the effort to profit by acquiring undervalued firms. Even absent competing bids, the information released after management's offer can raise the acquisition price enforced by the courts substantially above the prebid market price.

A commonly argued version of the asymmetric information view states that managers distort pre-MBO earnings to make the company appear unattractive, thereby enabling themselves to buy it for less. As a test of this view, Linda DeAngelo (1986) looked for abnormal earnings accruals prior to MBOs and found no evidence of significant misrepresentation of earnings.

It is very hard to say whether companies bought out by management are systematically underpriced. What we can say is that Value Line's 1980 write-ups of the twelve firms in our Fortune 500 MBO sample suggested that the share prices of many of these firms contained substantial room for appreciation. For example, Value Line thought that eight of our twelve companies had very good long-run capital gains prospects and that three out of twelve had moderately good long-run prospects. At the same time, Value Line did not think that short-term prospects were good for any of our companies. While the write-ups from Value Line hardly constitute strong evidence for irrational valuation by the market, they do suggest that these MBO targets were valued below their potential. Interpreted broadly enough, this observation may be hard to dispute, especially given the premia ultimately paid.

Efficiency Gains

Last but not least, we turn to a discussion of true value creation in MBOs, recognizing that the economic evaluation of the MBO turns crucially on the realization of efficiency gains. Both tax savings and buying underpriced shares from shareholders are examples of transfers of value between parties and not of true value creation. While such transfers change the distribution of the pie, they do not affect the size of the pie. The question of value creation is whether or not MBOs make the pie bigger.

In discussing value creation, the first thing to note is that the ownership and financial structure in MBOs is heavily geared toward providing managers with incentives to squeeze additional value out of the firm's assets. Such motivating arrangements come in three forms.

First, managers are given large equity stakes in their firms, which raise their personal benefit from improving efficiency. Lowenstein (1985) found in his sample of large MBOs that management's percentage ownership rises from a median 3.8 percent prior to the MBO to a median 10.4 percent after the transaction. The latter number is consistent with the finding of Mørck, Shleifer, and Vishny (1988) who, in a cross-section of public Fortune 500 firms, identified 5–10 percent as the range of management ownership associated with the best performing firms. MBOs thus give managers big enough percentage stakes to provide the right incentives, but not big enough to confer complete control.

In the vast majority of these cases, managers do not pay for these equity stakes out of their own pockets. In fact, they could not afford such investments in many instances. In most MBOs, managers are just given these large equity stakes for virtually no money.

While equity stakes seem to be given to the managers with the intention of motivating them to work hard, there is always the stick in addition to the carrot. As stressed in the free-cash-flow theory of Jensen (1986), the necessity to meet debt payments focuses the minds of managers on realizing the firm's full potential, since default and renegotiation can cost them their independence and possibly their jobs.

Last but not least, investment bankers usually also own a substantial amount of equity in the firm and are often capable of firing managers who are not performing as expected. It is conceivable that having an investment banker breathing down the manager's neck is as good a motivating device as equity ownership.

These last considerations may suggest why managers might not jump into MBOs without a hostile threat, despite the potential for large financial rewards. After an MBO, managers lose much of their control over free cash flows as well as the ability to run their firms without outside interference, for at least a few years. While it is good to be rich, it is also good to be free.

Granted that managers are motivated to improve operating efficiency, what can they actually accomplish? Although hard evidence is not abundant, belt-tightening measures typically seem to include the shortening of accounts receivable collection periods, decreasing inventory-to-sales ratios, insisting on better deals from suppliers, cutting capital expenditures, and cutting employment. (In a sample of 200 British firms, for example, the average employment cut was 18 percent subsequent to an LBO. This was not the result of management cuts, which were not very large. See Wright and Coyne 1985.) While some of these methods for increasing efficiency do not seem very revolutionary, it is important to realize that many of the target companies are in fairly competitive industries with low profit margins to start with. Small cost savings in these companies can add up to a vastly improved return on assets.

Norris Industries is one case for which we have information about some of the belt-tightening measures. After the MBO, Norris liquidated $50 million in inventory and stabilized at half of its pre-MBO inventory-to-sales ratio. It also required customers to pay their bills in forty rather than fifty-five days. Finally, Norris sold a division for $34 million, taking a $3 million write-off. While these measures undoubtedly created some value, the Norris case is interesting in that something beyond cost cutting was clearly going on. While the MBO transaction took place at approximately 1.6 times tangible book value, twenty-two months later Norris was reoffered to the public for approximately seven times book value. According to McGuire (1984), Norris is one of a group of companies going public in the hot new issues market of 1982–83 shortly after going private, whose huge successes were largely the result of paper transmutations, in other words, value transferred from old, and, particularly, new public shareholders.

The example of Norris is suggestive in that, although value creation may not have been the initial impetus for the MBO, nontrivial efficiency gains were nonetheless realized. Even when tax savings and the informational inefficiency of the market create the opportunities for large value transfers, the MBO deals that are ultimately struck are still structured so as to provide superior incentives for value creation.

5.2.5 Effects of Risk

The existence of tax savings, underpricing, or the potential for efficiency gains are not the only important characteristics of an MBO candidate. First, the increased financial risk incurred by the highly leveraged post-MBO firm means that business risk should be low. A company operating in an unstable environment in which its cash flows are subject to large fluctuations cannot take on 80–90 percent debt and still be fairly certain of meeting its regular payments. Furthermore, management's obsession with the financial side, along with limited access to new financing, make growth and concentration on areas such as product development and marketing quite difficult. If these areas are important sources of future profits, an MBO may be ill advised. Consistent with these limitations, MBOs typically occur in mature industries with stable cash flows, such as food and textiles. Of course, the step-up in basis for depreciation purposes can also be more dramatic for older firms which, as cash cows, are also more likely to offer large value gains from restricting management's access to free cash flows.

The requirement of stable cash flows to meet debt payments also explains the necessity of retaining the experienced incumbent management team, a strategy which is unlikely to bring a big positive surprise but is equally unlikely to bring a big negative surprise. It is the latter factor that matters for debt payments. The importance of the experience and continuity of the management team in an MBO may also help to account for the great deals that managers strike when equity is divided up.

While MBO organizers bear substantial risk, they also enjoy large upside potential. After the five to six years in which the debt is being repaid, the firm belongs to equity holders. Management in this case would typically own a 10–15 percent stake in a debt-free firm. If efficiency gains are realized, cash flows are likely to exceed the amount needed to meet debt payments. In a company operating with a substantial amount of slack prior to the buyout, these gains can be quite large. Finally, even if things do not work out, it is probably easier for a private company with substantial investment banker ownership to renegotiate its debts.

Many recent examples attest to the enormous gains to be made by organizers of leveraged buyouts. We have already mentioned the Norris example, in which assets bought for 1.6 times book were resold to the public for 7 times book value less than two years later. Two other striking examples are Converse and Gibson Greeting Cards. While these were "leveraged buyouts," they could not strictly be called "management buyouts" since both companies were purchased as divisions of public companies (Allied and RCA, respectively). Yet the huge profits made (returns to organizers were 5 to 1 in Converse and 200 to 1 in the Gibson case) were also likely to have been due in part to value transferred from public shareholders.

Just as exogenous circumstances brought on the MBOs in the early 1980s, exogenous circumstances also blessed them two years later. The new issues market has been especially hot, enabling MBO organizers who bought assets in the bear market of the very early 1980s to do quite well. While there is good reason to believe that MBOs have done well in part because they encouraged efficiency and in part because of tax breaks, there was also clearly a large element of luck involved.

5.3   Conclusion

Whether or not management buyouts are a good thing depends on whom you ask. To the investment bankers who earned both high fees and 50–60 percent annualized returns on their equity positions, MBOs were a good thing. To the shareholders who got out of poorly performing firms at a 50 percent premium, MBOs were probably a good thing, although they may have wished that they could have stayed on to receive a bigger portion of the tax and efficiency gains and, with the benefit of hindsight, to profit from the enormous rally in the new issues market. MBOs were probably also a good thing for managers who traded a good deal of sweat for valuable equity positions, and perhaps more important, for the opportunity to escape a hostile takeover. To the banks, MBOs were probably also a good thing, in contrast to many of their other above prime loans. The principal loser in MBOs may very well be the taxman who definitely paid for at least some of the profits made by everybody else.

Whether MBOs are a good thing from the economist's perspective depends on whether they promote economic efficiency. While it is likely that much of the premium and the impetus behind MBOs came from the existence of value transfer gains, the end result was clearly a nontrivial amount of value creation. The enterprises emerging from MBOs are invariably structured to give managers greater incentives to cut costs and to budget capital more responsibly. Increased management ownership, concentrated ownership in the hands of knowledgeable profit-motivated investment bankers, and reduced free cash flows all contribute to the value created in MBOs. Finally, managers who know their firms best get to keep them, and all of the upheaval costs associated with hostile takeovers are avoided. While there is no doubt that issues of fairness to various parties loom large in any view of management buyouts, from the point of view of promoting efficiency they appear to be a good thing.

Note

We would like to thank James Hines and Steve Kaplan for very helpful discussions and the National Bureau of Economic Research for research support.

References

Black, F. 1986. "Noise." *The Journal of Finance* 41 (July): 529–43.
DeAngelo, H., L. DeAngelo, and E. Rice. 1984. "Going Private: Minority Freezeouts and Stockholder Wealth." *Journal of Law and Economics* (October): 367–402.
DeAngelo, L. 1986. "Accounting Numbers as Market Valuation Substitutes: A Study of Management Buyouts of Public Stockholders." *The Accounting Review* (July): 400–420.
Feldstein, M. 1983. *Capital Taxation.* Cambridge: Harvard University Press.
Gordon, R., J. Hines, and L. Summers. 1986. "Notes on the Tax Treatment of Structures." NBER working paper, April.
Jensen, M. 1986. "Agency Costs of Free Cash Flow, Corporate Finance, and Takeovers." *American Economic Review.* Papers and Proceedings 76 (May): 326–29.
Lowenstein, L. 1985. "Management Buyouts." *Columbia Law Review* 85 (May): 730–84.
McGuire, R. 1984. "The Creation of Value in Management Leveraged Buyouts." In L. Ryder Mason. ed., *Structuring and Financing Management Buyouts: A Case History Digest,* San Diego: Buyout Publications.
Mørck, R., A. Shleifer, and R. Vishny. 1988. "Management Ownership and Market Valuation: An Empirical Analysis." *Journal of Financial Economics,* forthcoming.
Wright, M., and J. Coyne. 1985. *Management Buy-Outs.* London: Croom Helm.

Contributors

Alan J. Auerbach
Department of Economics
University of Pennsylvania
3718 Locust Walk/CR
Philadelphia, PA 19104

Devra L. Golbe
Department of Economics
Hunter College
695 Park Ave.
New York, NY 10021

David Reishus
U.S. Joint Committee on Taxation
1015 Longworth House Office
  Building
Washington, DC 20515

Richard S. Ruback
Sloan School of Management
Massachusetts Institute of
  Technology
E52-243A
Cambridge, MA 02139

Andrei Shleifer
Graduate School of Business
University of Chicago
1101 East 58th Street
Chicago, IL 60637

Robert A. Taggart, Jr.
School of Management
Finance/Economics Department
Boston University
704 Commonwealth Avenue
Boston, MA 02215

Robert W. Vishny
Graduate School of Business
University of Chicago
1101 East 58th Street
Chicago, IL 60637

Lawrence J. White
Federal Home Loan Bank Board
1700 G Street, NW
Washington, DC 20552

Index

Acquisitions: activity determinants, 40–41; benefits of, 69–70; break-up, 17; creeping, 60; data sources, 26–29; depreciation and, 73; dividend distribution, 72; historical patterns, 26–36; Internal Revenue Code and, 73; junk bond financing, 14–15; leverage and, 79–80; manufacturing and mining data, 75; market competition and, 69; potential gains, 93; prior stock issuances and, 84; service sector data, 29 stepped-up asset basis, 78–79; taxation and, 69 85 Tobin's q and, 40; waves, 36. *See also* Mergers; Takeovers
Allied, Inc., 100
Altman, E. I., 11
Assets: churning, 90; exchanges of, 40; inflation and, 89; as loan collateral, 13; mergers and, 30; restructuring, 64; stepped-up basis, 73, 78–79; stripping, 17; value creation, 97–99
Auerbach, Alan J., 73–74, 83

Banks. *See* Borrowing; Investment banking
Beatrice Foods, Inc., 25, 88
Becketti, S., 17
Belzberg family, 13
Bianco, A., 13
Black, F., 96
Blank check preferred stock, 58
Bleakley, F. R., 13

Board elections, 56–57
Bond: mutual funds, 11; ratings, 8. *See also specific type*
Borrowing: competition for, 7; corporate restructuring and, 19; junk bonds and, 10; mergers and, 79–80; taxation and, 74; unsecured debt, 91
Bradley, Michael, 61
Buyouts. *See* Leveraged buyouts; Management buyouts

Capital: internal funds for, 85 n. 3; markets, 6–8; real cost of, 41
Cash cows, 100
Charter provisions, 2
Churning, 90
Columbia Savings and Loan Association, 18
Commercial paper market, 6–7
Congoleum, Inc., 95
Converse, Inc., 100
Corporations: bond issues, 11; debt-equity increases, 16; shell, 13–14; sources of funds, 6. *See also specific corporations*
Coyne, J., 98
Creeping acquisitions, 60
Crown-Zellerbach, Inc., 60

Dann, Larry Y., 61, 63–64
Dan River, Inc., 95
DeAngelo, Harry, 57, 61, 63–64, 92, 96
DeAngelo, Linda, 92, 96

105